AF572099

Beautiful Michigan Volume II

Beautiful
Michigan
Volume II

Text by Louis Cook

Published by
Beautiful America Publishing Company
4720 S.W. Washington
Beaverton, Oregon 97005

Robert D. Shangle, Publisher

ISBN 0-915796-88-0 (paperback)
ISBN 0-915796-89-9 (Hardbound)

PHOTO CREDITS

GENE AHRENS—page 56.

MARILYN AMES SHUMAKER—page 14, above.

VICKI AMES—page 14, below.

WILLIAM BAKE—page 41.

ROY BISHOP—pages 12-13; page 19; pages 20-21; page 22, above; page 24; pages 32-33; pages 44-45; pages 48-49; page 50; page 52; page 55; page 57, below; page 60, above; page 61, above; page 61, below; page 64; page 65, above; page 65, below; page 68, below; page 72.

BOB EIKUM—page 50, above.

VIRGIL D. HAYNES—page 11, below; pages 16-17; page 18, above; page 18, below; page 25, below; page 36, above; page 36, below; page 40, above; page 43, above; page 43, below; page 46, below; page 53, below; page 54, above.

PATRICK OWEN—page 10; page 25, above; pages 28-29- page 42; page 46, above; page 51; page 57, above.

MICHIGAN DEVELOPMENT COUNCIL—page 22, below.

MICHIGAN TOURIST COUNCIL—page 47; page 54, above.

EDWIN SCHILLER—page 9; page 15; page 23; page 37; page 40, below; page 69.

JEFF TURNER—page 68, above.

CONTENTS

INTRODUCTION

The look of Michigan has been vastly transformed in the last 150 years, and a good case can be made for the idea that civilization has improved it in many ways. The early settlers made little comment, however, on how things looked. They were immersed in clearing land, building railroads, and surviving.

The kind of painters who gave us immortal vistas of the Hudson River in early times do not seem to have been attracted to Michigan, where indeed there would have been few to buy their works.

But we know a great deal about the look of the land from an adventurous French politician and lawyer, Alexis de Tocqueville, who visited Michigan in the summer of 1831 and deliberately sought out the wildest, most inhospitable and most uncomfortable area he could reach on foot or horseback. People thought he was crazy.

In his "Journey to America" de Tocqueville described his arrival in Detroit at 4 p.m. on July 22 and looking up Father Gabriel Richard, a Catholic priest who published the city's first newspaper and was one of the founders of the University of Michigan. Father Richard's coffin still reposes in Ste. Anne's Church in Detroit.

A land speculator tried to tout de Tocqueville toward areas in the state already under development, warning him that in the direction of Pontiac and Saginaw lay "impenetrable forest which stretched endlessly to the northwest, where one finds only wild beasts and Indians." That was what de Tocqueville was looking for. Hiring a horse and shouldering his double-barreled percussion cap rifle—an object of curiosity and envy in those times—he set out toward Pontiac.

De Tocqueville found himself in deep forest a mile after leaving the Detroit River. That would have put him just past Grand Circus Park in present-day Detroit. He would have journeyed down dirt roads that became the site of skyscrapers housing the financial center of Michigan.

He arrived in Pontiac after sundown: "Twenty very clean and very pretty houses . . . a transparent stream . . . and the everlasting forest all around." There were hotels in Pontiac—two, in fact—and the owner of the one de Tocqueville chose was incredulous when informed that the Frenchman intended to go to Saginaw.

"Do you know that Saginaw is the last inhabited point until you come to the Pacific Ocean? Do you know that from here you find hardly anything but wilds and untrod solitudes?" There was more, including reference to forest fever, a common and often fatal ailment among Michigan settlers who spent time in the damp and dark forest lands.

So de Tocqueville and a friend from France set out into the forest. His story of his experiences is an odd account, varying from poetic admiration of Michigan to abject terror.

Here's what he wrote following a canoe trip on the Saginaw River: ". . . a flowering solitude, delightful and scented; a magnificent dwelling, a living palace built for man . . . the serenity of universal calm reigned around us . . . we talked less and less and soon found we put our thoughts into whispers. Finally we fell silent and both of us fell into a tranquil reverie full of inexpressible charm."

And then: "At midday the sun darts its beams on the forest and one hears in its depths something like a long sigh, a plaintive cry lingering in the distance. It is the last stir of the dying wind. Then everything around you falls back into silence so deep, a stillness so complete that the soul is invaded by a kind of religious terror . . . the forest trees seem to form but one whole, immense and indestructible edifice under whose vaults eternal darkness reigns. On whatever side he looks, he sees nothing but a field of violence and destruction. Broken trees and torn trunks, everything testifies that the elements are here perpetually at war. All is still in the woods, all is silent under their leaves. One would say for a moment the Creator has turned his face away and all the forces of nature are paralyzed."

De Tocqueville's poetic insight into early Michigan and the people who inhabited various portions of it were all the more remarkable considering the distractions he encountered. Rattlesnakes abounded in the meadow grass along the streams, and then there were the mosquitoes: "By day they stopped us sketching, writing or staying one moment in the same place; by night they circled in their thousands around us . . . woken by the pain of their stings we covered our heads in the sheets, but their needles went through them . . ."

De Tocqueville made it back to Detroit safely, and took a steamer to Sault Ste. Marie, Bois Blanc and Mackinac Islands and on to Green Bay, Wisconsin. His accounts of his further Michigan travels were mostly concerned with Indians met along the way. Nothing stirred him quite as much as his days and nights in the deep forest.

And the forest was unusual. It was part of the great hardwood forest of the Ohio basin and covered all of what is now Michigan, except for a few cleared areas in the southwest corner, probably the sites of Indian cornfields. On the dry gravel lands were red, black and white oaks, hickory, ash, cherry, basswood and walnut. In the lowlands grew maple, elm, ash, beech and sycamore, poplar and willow. As the forest extended northward it began to include pine, tamarack and cedar.

It was wild and beautiful, but not very hospitable. Nature is an untidy housekeeper, and the Michigan de Tocqueville saw had lain largely undisturbed since the last Pleistocene glacier 18,000 years previously. It was a tangle of fallen trees, swamps, wild rivers and cockleburrs. Except on the open water there were few places to admire a sunset, and a fall color tour was out of the question.

There is risk in going too far in tidying up a howling wilderness. Now we are taking measures to save wild rivers as they dwindle to too few; to set aside forests for those coming after us. There have been excesses of exploitation, and people of Michigan are rousing to the threat.

But it is not too late. Michigan is a fair land, and will continue to be.

(Preceding page) Grebe Lake is one of hundreds of small bodies of water in Central Michigan.

(Opposite) Pine trees crowd close to the shore of Lake Superior, bearing the brunt of offshore winds.

(Right) Roses thrive in Michigan gardens during summer months.

(Below) Harbor Point Lighthouse has guided thousands of lakers home.

(Following pages) Fall color and a troubled sky over Bailey Lake suggest that the seasons' change is near.

(Third following page, above) The Sable River winds quietly through Ludington State Park to lose itself in Lake Michigan.

(Third following page, below) Piers on Lake Michigan are silhouetted sharply in day's last light.

(Fourth following page) A little-frequented road offers something of the feeling of a cathedral in the leafy canopy that arches overhead.

(Preceding pages) Tahquamenon Falls have roared for centuries in the lonely timberland west of Sault Ste. Marie.

(Left) Dewy raspberries are among the varieties of fruit for which Michigan is famous, especially in Berrien County.

(Below) Rock breakwaters protect the cottages on the sandy shores of Lake Michigan.

(Opposite) A new day breaks over the placid waters of Muskegon Lake.

(Left) The moods of Lake Superior are many, and not always peaceful, as this evening view near Copper Harbor suggests.

(Following page, above) At the far reach of a Shiawassee River lagoon can be seen the tower of Curwood Castle, in Owosso.

(Following page, below) Lake Michigan splashes up on the broad curve of a pebbled beach, with Sleeping Bear Dune in the background.

(Second following page) The wind-rippled surface of a Lower Peninsula lake fragments the colorful reflection of trees on the far bank, while falling leaves signal the end of a season.

(Third following page) Evening shadows deepen on the delta of Sand Creek where it empties into Lake Superior near Marquette.

THE NAMES OF MICHIGAN

The early settlers of Michigan did not leave many descriptions or paintings of the look of the land as they found it, but there are good clues as to their feelings in the names they placed on their new homes. There was a Mud River, and a few Crooked Lakes, but grubby and homely place names were, and are, few.

Beulah, in the dune country on the Lake Michigan side, was named for Beulah Land, flowing in milk and honey. Eureka—"I have found it!"—shows up three times, in one variation or another. There are nine uses of Pleasant, most of them Pleasant Valley.

There are several Richlands, and 14 communities named Rose Bush, Rose City, and other variations on a pretty flower. Silver Lake was popular, with nine plays on the theme. There was a Sweetland, a Sylvan Lake, and, of course, Willow Run.

A note of asperity was provided by the founding fathers of Yellow Jacket, but Zion was named after the Beautiful City of God. Bellaire was the pretty name chosen by the settlers of the community in Antrim County, and Agate and Alabaster were put on the map by their respective founders. The last two were named after mineral deposits in the area, but they have a pleasant ring.

Bloom was chosen for its fresh quality in a number of places: Bloomingdale, Bloomfield Hills, Blooming Grove and Blooming Valley. Hesperia was the neat poetic name chosen by residents of the new community in Oceana County, in Western Michigan. There are seven Crystal Lakes.

Many of the early settlers were French, and Belle (for beautiful) was popular, giving rise to Belle Isle, Belle River, Belleville and Bellevue and Belle Harbor. The same sort of thinking must have gone into the naming of the Beau River, in Emmet County.

(Preceding page, below) In many places in Michigan, virgin stands of white pine still raise their heads to the sun.

The local flora and fauna inspired many of the settlers, as might be expected. The names are possibly not as imaginative or flattering as some of the more poetic, but they have a pleasant sound.

Birch figures in four place names, Cedar crops up 21 times, Pine 22 times, Oak in 24 variations. Burr Oak, Butternut and Hemlock were chosen. Blackberry Ridge. Peach Ridge. Three Evergreens. Fern and two Ferndales. Four Bear Creeks. Fruitland. Fruitport. Eight Beaver Lakes. Bass Lake. Bass Beach. Bass Landing, Basswood and Basswood Corners, after the tree, of course.

And geography inspired many community fathers. Bay Port has eight variations in Michigan. There are 53 variations on "Lake." There's Limestone.

And then there was brave Sans Souci. Life in early Michigan is not known to have been carefree anywhere.

(Following pages) Winter is king at the Sturgeon River Falls, in Baraga County.

THE LOWLANDS

Michigan's lowlands stretch from Saginaw and the Thumb on the east to the dune country of Ludington and Pentwater on the west. In much of it, especially along the channel of an ancient glacial river that once transected Michigan from Saginaw Bay to the Grand Rapids area, the elevations are commonly less than 100 feet above Lakes Michigan and Huron. The Saginaw, Maple and Grand Rivers follow the old channel.

Since the visit of Alexis de Tocqueville 150 years ago, the lowlands have been mellowed by time, agriculture, logging, and an encrustation of foundries and factories. Not all of this has been for the better, but not all for the worse, either. The uplands further north are better known for their natural beauty, but the lowlands contain some of the state's greatest treasures in gracious towns and unusual and lovely traces of what Michigan was like before the white man came.

In Calhoun County, toward Lake Michigan, is a tract bounded by a railroad and Helmer Brook that has never known a plow or grazing livestock. It is undisturbed virgin prairie, where still grow pink-plumed Queen-of-the-Prairie, seldom seem any more. And, of course, Indian Tobacco, Queen Anne's Lace, and other more familiar open country growth.

Michigan has its own stand of American Lotus. The last patch in the state is in Monroe County, near Lake Erie and north of Toledo, Ohio. The pale cream lotus blooms appear in early August in the Swan Creek Estuary near Lake Erie. The place is also home to False Dragonhead, Mallow and Iris, and is populated by ducks, egrets and herons.

The construction of Interstate Highway I-94 has deprived travelers of the charms along the old U.S. 12 route from Detroit to Chicago, although the swelling rises of the Irish Hills can be seen on the new route. But old U.S. 12 is still there, a two-laner with much local traffic but still the best vantage from which to take in a section of Michigan rich in history and scenery.

Saline. Jonesville. Coldwater, where a battery of Parrott guns stands still by the courthouse where the artillery company left them after the Civil War. Sturgis. Niles. Three Oaks. It is a land of country churches, Grange halls, and old courthouses standing in their old squares, surrounded by clipped lawns and venerable oaks.

The memorials to the Civil War dead stand with those of the Spanish-American War, World Wars I and II, Korea and Vietnam, and people still talk about Chickamauga and Gettysburg. Time moves deliberately here, and the old is treasured. The old Livingston County courthouse in Howell was recently restored to its original blue and gold interior, the doors and louvered shutters redone, the oil paintings on the vault doors cleaned. It also received a new heating system and air-conditioning.

Marshall was described some years ago as "an outstanding example of gracious dignity and Greek Revival architecture in America." Still one of the most beautiful homes in Michigan is the old Harold Brooks mansion, fronted by five Ionic columns two stories high that were hauled from Detroit by oxen in 1840. The side streets in nearby Charlotte have not changed much in a century . . . freshly painted Victorian gingerbread trim, the remnants of an old mill dam, beans bursting from the backyard gardens in the spring, gnarled lilacs in fragrant bloom, porch swings and picket fences.

A century ago the lowland cities grew around dams and mills that ground grain and powered saws and machinery. At Manchester the old mill still grinds chicken and pig feed a half block from the town's main street. The old mill at Hodunk—there really is a town with such a name—did not rest for more than 108 years. It is no longer in use, but the old mill stream is one of the loveliest places in Michigan.

Water was important to Owosso, too, where author James Oliver Curwood built a castle on the banks of the Shiawassee north of the old mill race and pond, a gracious place of drooping willows and tranquil pools. The dam at Grand Rapids, in the center of downtown, recently was bypassed by a fish ladder nationally acclaimed for its sculptural merit.

Weather and soil have much to do with the varying look of the lowlands. The prevailing winds are westerly on the western portion of the lowlands, and the stabilizing influence of Lake Michigan prevents rapid changes in temperature, making Berrien County, in the southwest, ideal for strawberries, and the rest of the Michigan shore excellent for growing peaches, apples and pears. And, further north in

(Left) In the Upper Peninsula, Bond Falls tumble down their rocky escarpment with wild abandon, to the tranquility of the pool below.

the Traverse City neighborhood, is the world's largest center of tart cherries.

The climate is much different further north, where the prevailing wind is northwesterly and not tempered by lake water. Upper Peninsula temperatures range from 108 above to 48 below zero. Subzero weather is rare lower down, and when it comes it is slow enough setting in to avoid tree damage.

The southeast section of the lowlands, in Lenawee and Monroe Counties, is a dark clay loam that is Michigan's closest approach to the fertile lands of Illinois and Iowa. This is corn-hog land, a surprise to those who know best the lighter soils further upstate. Here the precious land is farmed right to the roads, and fences are few. Feeder cattle and hogs are finished off in enclosed feedlots and barns. Lenawee has more than 2,000 farms with an average value of more than $70,000. Monroe has a few less, but the average value is several thousand dollars higher.

North of Detroit, in the area known as the Thumb, lies an entirely different type of soil, but equally rich. It is Brookston loam, a heavy clay soil wringing wet from Lake Huron. An on-shore wind raises the water level in the drainage ditches four feet.

Here the land lies flat as one's palm up through Utica, Bad Axe, and ending at Grindstone City, a unique place where grindstones were once cut from the rock and widely used industrially. The invention of the emery wheel and carborundum ended the city's manufacturing career, but the discarded grinding wheels, often six feet across, still line the old harbor, and the fishing is good.

The heavy wet soil is good for sugar beet culture and $21 million worth of sugar is produced in a good year. The mammoth, gray sugar mills dot the countryside. The Michigan navy bean is a big Thumb crop, as is wheat, the soft variety that is used in pies and pastry.

The lowlands further west are rich in deep mucklands, produced by decaying vegetation in the beds of old lakes and rivers. Michigan has one of the greatest supplies of peat in the United States, a resource as yet untapped but one that may prove important as the energy problem becomes more difficult.

The mucklands are important to growing onions, celery, potatoes, and carrots and root crops of all kinds. One of the most unusual farms in the state is the old Mentha plantation near Kalamazoo that is one of the principal sources in the United States for mint oil. The breeze across the fields on a hot July afternoon is delicious.

The farming of winter wheat in Michigan provides one of the great contributions to the look of things. The wheat is hardy and is usually sowed in the fall. By November the fields are greening into a soft, undulating comforter so lovely and enticing it is a temptation to roll in, an emerald sweep that goes out to the horizon.

Even after the leaves fall, and the sedges brown in the lakes, winter wheat keeps Michigan beautiful.

(Following page, above) Late rays of a setting sun brighten the clouds over quiet Lake Michigan.

(Following page, below) Draped with the lines by which it was hauled from the water, a lake boat waits out another winter.

THE UPLANDS

For many years following the turn of the century, Michigan's uplands, roughly north of a line drawn from Saginaw to Ludington, lay in quiet following the boisterous days of the lumber harvest that left large areas of the state a wasteland. With some exceptions it became resort country, jumping in summer when the fishing was good, and thronging with red-shirted hunters during the November deer season ritual.

But with the coming of winter's iron season, the tourists departed. Saks Fifth Avenue maintained a swank shop in Petoskey, as did many other firms well known in high fashion circles, but in winter the staff was transferred to a Florida shop that was closed in summer. Cheboygan and Charlevoix, both with a long history of catering to wealthy sportsmen and their families, fell silent, the yachts cradled under canvas on the shore or sailed back to home country.

There was upland activity of a special sort. The limestone quarries at Rogers City and Alpena, on the Lake Huron side, kept going most of the year, the long lakers snaking into port at all hours of the day and night. As the navigation season was extended, they faced 12-foot seas and 45-knot winds to move the stuff to the mills at Detroit and Toledo and Cleveland and Buffalo.

"A mud puddle," said a contemptuous French naval officer who took three destroyers into Lake Huron for refitting in Chicago during World War I. They never arrived, and no trace of them has ever been found. The Great Lakes are moody and dangerous. From the days of The Griffon, lost in the straits of Mackinac early in the history of the Northwest Territory, to the Edmund Fitzgerald, the most recent tragedy, the lakes have been widow and orphan makers. "The widows of the wind," a Detroit newspaperman once described the survivors of lost lakers finishing out lonely lives in the coastal towns.

But even the mighty locks at Sault Ste. Marie, to aid the lakers in transferring from Lake Superior, via Whitefish Bay and St. Mary's River, to Lake Huron 21 feet below, have been closed during the frigid weather

(Preceding page) The Hartwick Pines area in north central Michigan is still virgin timber land.

of January and February, although attempts to keep ship traffic open 12 months of the year are increasing.

The snow begins arriving in November and by Christmas it lies deep. For years the main highway from Grayling to the Mackinac Bridge was often just a wavering single track where traffic was bumper to bumper a few months previously. And then came the awakening. Snow. Maybe it was good for something, after all.

The land from the Leelanau Peninsula southward was hilly, almost mountainous. Boyne Mountain was one of the first to be developed into a ski resort, and many others followed rapidly. Caberfae. Nub's Nob, Crystal Mountain, Shanty Creek. The Upper Peninsula was ahead of them, however. The ski runs at Iron Mountain and Ishpeming have a long history, dating back to the days when adventurous Finns established the early ski jump records calling for them to leap off the runs and land flat at the end. Ski runs with a downhill landing slope came later. But the Iron Mountain and Ishpeming runs did not come into their own until lower Michigan loaded up on skis and wax, apres-ski attire, car-roof carriers and snowmobiles, and headed north pell-mell in the depths of winter, the worse the weather the better.

The uplands had been popular for a century as a place to build summer cabins along the lakes and streams. With the coming of ski and snowmobile fever, the more suitable areas have blossomed out in condominiums, motels and year-round homes. The snowmobile has made access to remote cabins and homes easy after many years when it was impossible to get people and supplies in.

The armies of backpackers and cross-country skiers are growing. With one exception, Michigan's uplands are available to any takers all year. The parks are often crammed to capacity. The sale and maintenance of motor homes and campers have become big business.

The exception, and a charming one, is Isle Royale National Park, located off the Keweenaw Peninsula in the extreme northern tip of the state. Here outcroppings of pure copper are still visible, mined by Indians and trappers in the early days for arrow points and hatchets. A

(Following page, above) Clouds close in over Lake Michigan as afternoon sun highlights the rocky shore.

(Following page, below) Forest meets farm amid a blaze of autumn color on the Lower Peninsula.

(Preceding page) Delicate Queen Anne's Lace punctuates the greens of springtime on the banks of the Platte River.

(Opposite) Sedges echo the gold of the changing birches along this autumnal Michigan lakeshore.

(Right) Three young white-tailed fawns pause for lunch in a remote meadow.

(Below) Michigan residents drive hundreds of miles to see the fall colors. This is journey's end at Harbor Springs.

(Following pages) The Black River roars through the narrow stone channel at Conglomerate Falls.

(Third following page, above) Delicate birches frame Bete Gris Bay, in Keweenaw County.

(Third following page, below) Swirls of sand and ice decorate the wintry shoreline of Lake Michigan, near the Manistique Lighthouse.

(Fourth following page) White-trunked birches, leaves golden from autumn's chill, crowd close to the shore of a peaceful Michigan lake.

(Previous pages) High in the Porcupine Mountains is Lake of the Clouds, a mountain tarn, with the Escarpment looming above.

(Left) A lone bird raises its voice in song in a quiet Michigan marsh.

(Below) Eroded by millions of years of sun and storm, Miner's Castle juts out into Lake Superior from the Pictured Rocks.

(Opposite) These are the hills of home in autumn, sumac afire in the tall grass and late sun catching the maples.

(Opposite) The Ambassador Bridge at Detroit is one of the few spans linking the United States with Canada. The others are the Blue Water, at Port Huron, and the lock bridges at the Soo.

(Right) Graceful flowers bedeck Michigan gardens in the summertime.

(Below) Settlers named Big Rock, near Five Mile Creek, a monolith that has resisted the waves for centuries.

(Following page, above) Visitors at Grand Marais are warned to keep off the breakwater during heavy weather, when wind-driven waves top the barrier with ease.

(Following page, below) Autumn color seems to explode along the banks of the tranquil Crystal River.

(Second following page) In spite of its lighthouse, Point Tawas is a graveyard for ships lost in violent lake storms.

(Third following page) Lake Superior is the largest fresh-water lake in the world, and its shoreline is witness to its furies.

National Park service boat is the main access to Isle Royale, but it is a long and cold ride from Houghton, and some travel back and forth by sea plane.

The federal government is working hard to keep Isle Royale a wilderness, to the extent of removing even the rude shelters erected years ago to keep the rain off hikers. There are inns at each end of the island, 26 miles apart, but between them a traveler is limited to whatever resources can be carried on one's back.

But the solitude and beauty are worth it. Birds perch unafraid on the toes of resting hikers, looking them over curiously. The main trail follows the spine of the island, with lovely vistas of forests falling away on either side to the waters of Lake Superior, the largest body of fresh water in the world, and the purest.

The island supports a moose herd, animals who came to the island by swimming over from the Canadian shore. They are no problem except during their rutting season, when it is wise to keep a tree between the hiker and the moose.

There are two small wolf packs on Isle Royale, but they are seldom seen, and then only in the winter, when researchers keep track of them by airplane. Purdue University made extensive studies of the wolf population, an activity that has been taken over in recent years by the University of Michigan.

But the season is short. On an August late afternoon one can see one's breath. By Labor Day the toughest backpacker is willing to put away his sleeping bag and alcohol burner and leave the island to the wolves and moose until mid-June of the next year. The two inns are closed up, and the storms take over.

In the early days of Isle Royale an attempt was made to colonize it. A field known as the Daisy Farm marks an ambitious try at agriculture on Isle Royale, but nothing grew there but daisies. It is a popular resting place for hikers, and the daisies are still there. But those who tried to winter over on Isle Royale had grim tales to tell the following spring, those of them that survived. Nobody has tried it for many years.

(Preceding page, above) Spring comes slowly to Mosquito Harbor Point, where the ice of a wild winter still clings to the shore ledges.

(Preceding page, below) The corn is ripe and autumn clouds hang low over a farm in The Thumb.

The uplands are home for a majority of the state's Indian population. Peshawbestown is an Indian town located near Traverse City on the Leelanau Peninsula, a land of silver lakes and quiet forests. Near Northwood is the Ottawa Cemetery, where lie buried Indian veterans of the nation's wars from that of 1812 to Korea. There are many Chippewas in the Soo area, and many work at ancient crafts during the summer at St. Ignace. Probably the greatest Indian population, however, is on the Cass Corridor in Detroit, where thousands of Indians are having a difficult time adapting themselves to western ways.

One of Michigan's best-known communities on a national scale is the little town of Pellston, located a few miles south of Mackinaw City, on a sandy area that radiates heat in the winter time so rapidly that it is one of the coldest places in the nation, on a par with a similar geological situation at Sparta, Wisconsin, where a temperature of 53 degrees below zero has been recorded on a number of occasions.

But residents of Pellston, as well as other communities in the uplands, are accustomed to having snow to the eaves and bears walking down the middle of the street. That means the snow birds from Detroit, Lansing and Grand Rapids will be along soon, putting traffic on the highways and shoppers in the stores.

The uplands are pretty in the summer . . . mile upon mile of greenery, interspersed with magnificent lakes. Torch and Houghton, the latter named for a Michigan geologist and naturalist who was drowned while making a field trip on Lake Superior in the mid-nineteenth century, are the biggest, but there are hundreds of handsome smaller bodies of open water.

One of the state's loveliest rituals is the annual color tour, when residents from all over the state go north to see the maples and birches in their last burst of flaming splendor before winter sets in. The uplands are the best viewing.

And then comes winter. Travel is through forest and sedge, in calm weather a reverent hush of sleeping nature, in a storm a rushing fury of savage beauty in which the jack pines and poplars moan against a darkling sky and the friendly lights of the next town guide the traveler to sanctuary.

(Following page) St. Stephen's Lutheran Church is near Silver Lake Park.

THE HIGHLANDS

Michigan residents usually consider as high ground the area including the Porcupine Mountains at the western end of the Upper Peninsula, toward the Wisconsin border. Geologically and from a standpoint of scenery, however, a fat strip of land stretching from Hillsdale, near the Ohio border, to Lapeer County, north and west of Detroit, is also highland, ranging from 1,000 to 1,600 feet above sea level and providing ski slopes within easy reach of the thickly populated areas of southeastern Michigan.

The Irish Hills country of lower Michigan is indeed a lovely area of green folds of land carpeting the hills worn by the glaciers of the Pleistocene era. But for wild, primeval beauty they do not match the Porcupines, the largest stand of hardwood-hemlock in the United States, a natural laboratory where one is not permitted to fell a tree, throw away a sardine tin, or even pick the flowers.

The Porcupines stretch for 60,000 acres along the Lake Superior shore, named that because from the lake the area resembled a hunched-up porcupine. One of its features is the Escarpment, a frowning wooded ridge that rises to 1,958 feet and is the highest land mass in the northern United States between the Black Hills and the Adirondack Mountains.

Hanging on to the Porcupines has been difficult. Loggers and miners have long coveted the timber, and the copper ore locked in their vitals. If the place were ever to be given over to commercial interests, including those who would like to build roads through it, erect motels, and cash in on its beauties, there would be, as a University of Wisconsin naturalist put it: ". . . an end of hardwood wilderness large enough for a day's skiing or hiking without crossing a road . . . an end of cathedral aisles to echo the hermit thrush or to awe the intruder . . . an end of the best schoolroom for foresters to learn what remains to be learned about hardwood forestry. We know little, and understand only a part of what we know."

(Preceding page, above) A sense of mystery still pervades much of the Keweenaw Peninsula, which was considered sacred land by local Indians.

(Preceding page, below) From Empire Bluffs the land slopes down to Lake Michigan and Sleeping Bear Lake.

From the Escarpment one looks down on a genuine mountain tarn, Lake of the Clouds, a glimmering blue expanse of water from which the Carp River emerges to drop 1,000 feet in 14 miles, almost a continuous plunge of wild rapids. Government Peak rises 1,850 feet above sea level, reached by a trail bordered with red elderberries and white-blossomed thimbleberries, rare except in the Porcupines.

The Porcupines are laced with wild rivers . . . the Big and the Little Carp, Pinkerton Creek, Union River, Lost Creek. Mirror Lake is correctly named.

The Porcupines are only a few miles fron Ontonagon, where the world's largest nugget of free-floating copper was discovered by the early settlers of Michigan. It weighs three tons and was an object of veneration for Indians traveling from Wisconsin to the Soo. They often camped in the wooded dell by a creek where the enigmatic piece of metal had brooded for thousands of years.

It was moved from the site by enterprising men who laid sections of railroad track ahead of it and manhandled the object to the shore of Lake Superior, where it was loaded on a boat. The Ontonagon Boulder now reposes in the Smithsonian Institution, but was brought to Detroit recently to be shown at a mineralogical exposition. Elaborate precautions were taken to prevent the boulder's being hijacked, an action proposed for years by Upper Peninsula Indians and legislators.

The Keweenaw and Marquette Highlands that include the Porcupines, and also Isle Royale, are approached by the high country around Cadillac, in the Lower Peninsula. Here also the traveler is surrounded by rugged hills with pines stretching to the sky; cold, clear brooks splashing down gravel and rocks to lose themselves in the lakes, wild stretches of timber and swamp known only to deer and badger.

The highest point in Michigan is not the mass of the Escarpment, however, although it is not far distant. To the east and north, toward Marquette, is Mt. Curwood, in the Huron Mountains, with an altitude of 1,980 feet.

The Upper Peninsula in the highland area is a rugged land exhibiting geologic formations that extend back to the Precambrian period, 570 million years ago, covering 87 per cent of known geologic time.

(Following page) Fayette, a ghost town, occupies a slender spit of land on Lake Michigan.

One of the most interesting evidences of the Cambrian is the Jacobsville sandstone at the approaches to the Keweenaw Peninsula, so ancient that it contains no fossils, predating the formation of life on earth.

It was during that era that the Upper Peninsula was a sea bottom, and a thick layer of sand was deposited. Down the ages this became compressed and indurated into sandstones that are visible in the famous Pictured Rocks National Lakeshore, on Lake Superior north and east of Munising.

The famous outcroppings were objects of superstitious dread to the Indians. Even today, when the sun is reflected on their changing colors above the restless waves of Lake Superior, the Pictured Rocks are an awesome reminder that human life is short, and that nature endures.

Another venerable bit of scenery in the area is the plant preserve between Eagle Harbor and Copper Harbor on the northern tip of the Upper Peninsula mainland. On the lake side is a harsh moonscape of puddingstone rocks, rounded pebbles cemented together by intense pressure down through the ages.

But on the sheltered inland side grow some of Michigan's rarest plants, including the butterwort, an explosion of color in the inhospitable cracks and pockets of Dan's Point, where Michigan ends.

(Preceding page, above) Covered bridges were covered to protect their timbers from the ravages of weather. This one is on the Flat River, near Grand Rapids.

(Preceding page, below) Deepening evening shadows are highlighted by reflections of the changing trees in Gun Lake, Yankee Springs State Park.

THE VALLEYS

Valleys have always had a powerful hold on people's imaginations, celebrated in story and song— "Red River Valley," "How Green Was My Valley," "Down In the Valley"—and rightly so. Valleys bring up mental images of fertile hillsides, cool streams and civilization.

The valleys were the first homes of man . . . the Nile, the Euphrates, the Rhone, the Yangtze, the Ganges. From the Detroit River, which is not really a river, the settlements spread along the Saginaw River, the Raisin, the Huron, and, on the western side of the state, the Grand, the Kalamazoo and the St. Joseph.

The Saginaw basin is one of the largest in Michigan, including four tributaries in the east central area that are rich in history, fertile soil and prosperous communities: The Tittabawasee, the Shiawassee, Flint and Cass Rivers. It adjoins the Grand River basin and its tranquil streams, a family that extends clear across the state to Lake Michigan; streams with pretty names or exciting ones: The Rogue, the Flat, Maple, Looking Glass, Red Cedar and Thornapple Rivers.

The Shiawassee owes much to James Oliver Curwood, the author of "The Flaming Forest" and many other popular novels, who grew up along its banks and made his home in Owosso, within earshot of its murmurs. He originated a conservation campaign that resulted eventually in the old Michigan Stream Pollution Commission embarking on an extensive river cleanup that made it the pleasant stream it is now.

Owosso has had its share of excitement down the years. When the state capitol was moved from Detroit in 1848, Owosso missed becoming the new site by one vote. Lansing, of course, prevailed. Owosso was the boyhood home of Tom Dewey, and for a time had dreams of being the first Michigan city to rear a president. Former President Gerald Ford lived in Grand Rapids, but was born in Omaha. Owosso even won the world's championship in indoor baseball, beating the Chicago Spaldings.

(Following page, above) The evening lights come on in downtown Detroit, with Renaissance Center on the right.

(Following page, below) Cottonwoods grow in the sands of Sleeping Bear dune.

The town was known as Big Rapids when it was settled in 1836 but the present name was adopted in 1875. The name came from Chief Wasso, whose tribe moved from the area to a reservation after the signing of the treaty of 1836.

The Shiawassee flows near Durand, another community that figures large in Michigan history, first as a coal mining center and then for its railroad activity. It was the intersection point of the Detroit and Muskegon branch of the Grand Trunk Western and the Ann Arbor Railroad.

An elephant is buried beside the old tracks, victim of a circus train wreck. Rail traffic is down, now, and the magnificent old depot is not used. But a railroad museum has been developed near it to keep memories of the old days alive.

Corunna, just upstream from Owosso, is an agricultural center and the home of Michigan's only manufacturer of brick. It also is the county seat, and is distinguished for its beautiful old county court house.

And just downstream from Owosso is Chesaning, the home of the famous Chesaning Showboat, an 80-foot craft that toots up to a 6,000-seat riverfront stadium to unload topflight "name" entertainers plus acts like the Kit Kats comedy dancers, and Gaby, Fofo and Miliki, musical comedians. Chesaning is Indian for "Big Rock."

Another charming town, down toward the Looking Glass River, is Perry, established in 1850 and named for Oliver Hazard Perry, the victor of the Battle of Lake Erie—"We have met the enemy and they are ours." At that time there were still many in Michigan who remembered the 1813 engagement first-hand.

One of the prettiest spots on the Grand River is at Grand Ledge, a small community just west of Lansing, where the river winds quietly through strata of sandstone and trees that give the place its name, a lovely setting for a straw-hat summer playhouse.

But the Grand is at its most spectacular when it swings north and west in a loop around Grand Rapids and booms south through the heart of the city, directly alongside the Vandenberg Center, scene of a yearly art fair that continues for days, and a successful experiment in city rebuilding.

(Preceding page) Sandstone ledges millions of years old line the Lake Superior approaches to the Porcupine Mountains.

Grand Rapids is no longer dependent on furniture manufacturing for its prosperity, but is more diversified, an important center for the arts, and famous for its gracious old homes. The Herman Miller Co. is in nearby Zeeland, however, keeping up the area's tradition for manufacturing high-quality furniture. The popular—and expensive—Charles Eames catcher's-mitt chair is produced there, all careful hand work, and contemporary rosewood chests that are becoming collector's items.

Valleys have always been important to wine makers, the slopes leading to the streams well-drained and fertile, as well as sheltered by surrounding hills. In Europe the valleys of the Rhine and the Rhone are celebrated for their bouquets, and in Michigan the activity is centered around Paw Paw, on the Paw Paw River south and west of Kalamazoo.

In addition to standard wines, Fenn Valley specializes in fruit wines from the pears, peaches, plums, strawberries and cherries that are important crops in Berrien County and other areas along Lake Michigan. Vendramino is the newest fermenter in the Paw Paw neighborhood, opening in an abandoned cider mill in 1977.

The Paw Paw River is a tributary of the St. Joseph along with the Dowagiac, Portage and Coldwater, all streams that wind through lush valleys heavy in harvest time with corn, soy beans, fruit and garden produce. Back from the freeways they are dreamy, quiet refuges where Holsteins and Brown Swiss graze and anglers cast out their lines.

Further up Lake Michigan the valley of the Pere Marquette is the scene of a wild canoe race yearly down to Ludington, where the Pere Marquette empties into the dune country. The valley of the Au Sable, in northeastern Michigan, is heavily traveled by canoe voyageurs in the summer, but is left to the deer, the otter and the muskrat when winter closes in.

The valleys of the Upper Peninsula are less accessible, although the Tahquamenon has many visitors every year to inspect its famous falls, and the Two-Hearted River was immortalized by Ernest Hemingway.

(Following page) Black River Park is the place to witness unforgettable Lake Superior sunsets.

HISTORY & TECHNIQUES OF THE

Great Masters

MANET

HISTORY & TECHNIQUES OF THE

Great Masters

MANET

Linda Bolton

CHARTWELL BOOKS, INC.

A QUANTUM BOOK

Published by Chartwell Books
A Division of Book Sales Inc.
114 Northfield Avenue
Edison, New Jersey 08837
USA

This edition printed 2003

ISBN 0-7858-1641-0

QUMMAN

This book is produced by
Quantum Publishing Ltd.
6 Blundell Street
London N7 9BH

Printed in China by Leefung-Asco Printers Ltd.

Contents

The Paintings

Introduction

Henri Fantin-Latour
Portrait of Edouard Manet
1867, Chicago Art Institute

Modern art begins with Manet. His legacy to the latter half of the 19th century affected every artist of note, and as Renoir said, for the Impressionists he was what Giotto or Cimabue were for the artists of Renaissance. To the generation that succeeded him Manet seemed to have invented an entirely new kind of painting, completely breaking away from the earlier tradition of depicting the external world accurately within the accepted style of the day. Manet claimed to paint what he saw, but he introduced two elements that were to alter the history of painting for ever. The first was the transformation of the image into a highly personal vision, entirely at odds with the contemporary style, and the second was the recognition of the essential artifice of painting, which was also stressed by Edgar Degas. This was put into words by another artist, Maurice Denis, in 1890. "Remember that a picture — before being a warhorse, a nude woman or an anecdote — is essentially a flat surface covered with colors assembled in a certain order."

The new art

Manet's new approach encouraged other artists, particularly the Impressionists, to consciously interpret their sensations of nature, instead of merely reproducing an image with the greatest possible degree of accuracy. It also led to an entirely new way of seeing the role of painting, so that subsequent generations could acknowledge it as an autonomous and personal art form rather than a vehicle for public preaching, edification or storytelling. After Manet, a painting could be whatever the artist chose it to be.

By the middle of the 19th century both artists and writers had become increasingly aware that a new direction was needed in art. Painting had become sterile and irrelevant to modern life, and the poet Théophile Gautier spoke for many when he said that "Today art has at its disposal only dead ideas and formulas which no longer correspond to its need. Something must be done, but what?" A similar sentiment was expressed by Victor Hugo after the revolution of 1848. "Poor great France, unconscious and blind! It knows what it does not want, but does not yet know what it does want." The poet Charles Baudelaire, later to become Manet's close friend, shared this sentiment. "The great tradition is lost," he said, "and a new one not yet created."

Manet took on the role of pathfinder, pointing the way forward by rejecting the academicism instilled by traditional teaching. He painted, not historical or mythological subjects, but the world he saw around him. His technique, like his subject matter, broke all previously accepted rules: he radically rethought methods of composition, handling of color and tone, brushwork and the treatment of light. His paintings, with their acid, often disconcerting juxtapositions of strong color, their harsh lighting and elimination of half-tones, bold brushstrokes, absence of detail, deliberate flattening of form and inconsistencies of scale, combined with his choice of subject matter to outrage the gallery-going public. People were accustomed to highly "finished" works, in which colors were subtly blended together, brushwork was so smooth as to be virtually invisible, and nudes were given respectability by appearing in the guise or nymphs from classical myth or figures in biblical narrative. One has only to compare Cabanel's highly acclaimed *Birth of Venus* (opposite) with Manet's *Déjeuner sur l'herbe* (see page 25) to see the difference between the old art and the new.

Student years

Edouard Manet, the eldest of three sons, was born into the cultured Parisian bourgeoisie; his father was a prominent magistrate in the Ministry of Justice and his mother, the daughter of a diplomat, was an amateur musician. His father's first wish was for his son to follow his own footsteps into the legal profession, but the young

EDOUARD MANET
Self-portrait after Tintoretto
1854, Musée de Dijon

Manet's earliest known works are copies of the Old Masters. His teacher Thomas Couture guided his students towards the painterly techniques of artists such as Titian, Tintoretto, Velasquez and Delacroix. Manet considered Tintoretto's self-portrait the most beautiful portrait in the world, and always stopped before it in the Louvre.

Manet's enthusiasm for drawing had led to a neglect of his studies, and his scholastic record was indifferent. The second option was a career in the navy, but after failing two sets of naval exams Manet succeeded in persuading his father to let him study art.

In 1851 he entered the studio of Thomas Couture, a portrait and history painter, whom he had chosen in preference to the prestigious but stultifyingly academic Ecole des Beaux Arts. Unfortunately he found little inspiration with his chosen master, and studied under him with increasing frustration for six years. As at the Beaux Arts, the students were set to copy plaster casts of classical statuary, and when professional models were hired they were arranged in exaggeratedly heroic poses.

"Everything we are given to look at is ridiculous," Manet complained. "The light is false, the shadows are false. When I arrive at the studio I feel as if I were entering a tomb." A fellow student, Antonin Proust, described a quarrel with one of the male models. "What! Can't you be more natural?" Manet shouted at the naked man. "Is that the way you would buy a bunch of radishes at the greengrocers?" The model, choking with anger, reminded Manet that it was thanks to him that several artists had won the Prix de Rome, the highest and most coveted award, which gave young artists the opportunity of studying in Rome at the French Academy. Manet's retort – "We're not in Rome now and we don't want to go there. We're in Paris; let's stay here" – reveals his scorn for the blind acceptance of classically inspired tradition. A thoroughgoing Parisian, he sought inspiration from his own city, not from rules dictated by academies. "It's only too easy," he said, "to accept ready made formulas, to bow

ALEXANDRE CABANEL
Birth of Venus
1862, Musée d'Orsay, Paris

Highly acclaimed by the Salon of 1863, this painting exemplifies the type of titillating nude, painted in a polished and highly finished style, appreciated by the gallery-going public in the mid-19th century. The eroticism of this Venus was acceptable because it was given respectability by the classical framework, while Manet's *Déjeuner sur l'herbe* (see page 25), exhibited the same year, was found shocking both in style and in content.

DIEGO VELASQUEZ
Las Meninas
1656, Prado, Madrid

Manet had a lifelong admiration for Velasquez, calling him "the painter to beat all painters." He described this work as an "extraordinary picture," and wrote that "I have found in the work of Velasquez the realization of my ideal in painting." He borrowed Velasquez' somber tonalities and his use of luminous blacks and grays, also imbuing his own canvases with the apparent spontaneity of the master's work.

down before what's called 'ideal classical beauty,' as though beauty were something constant. Beauty, of course is always changing . . . beauty is something malleable."

Unlike the majority of painters, Manet realized his personal style at an early age. Proust recalled the remark of a fellow student at Couture's that "There's a fellow called Manet who does some astonishing work but doesn't get on with the models." Even his earliest works show a boldness of composition and handling, with a preference for the single figure and a liking for the somber, dramatic arrangements of Tintoretto, Le Nain, Velasquez and Goya. But although he was admired by the students, he was a source of irritation to his master. On one occasion Couture, upbraiding him for posing the model in his own clothes instead of naked, and in a naturalistic rather than heroic pose, told him he would never be more than the Daumier of his day. Manet replied that he would rather be a Daumier (a painter of everday subject matter, a cartoonist and social satirist) than a Coypel (an 18th-century history painter).

The Parisian dandy

Manet spoke little and wrote less about his art, but it is a testimony to his culture, wit and intelligence that he was the intimate of three of the century's greatest literary figures, the poets Charles Baudelaire and Stéphane Mallarmé and the novelist Emile Zola. It is from Baudelaire, whom Manet had met by 1858, that we learn most about the artist, and he is often seen as Manet's spokesman, particularly in what he called the "heroism of modern life." The cult of the dandy, the stroller on the boulevard and frequenter of cafés, concealing his life of the imagination beneath an urbane and immaculate exterior, was also extolled by Baudelaire and practiced by Manet.

The young Manet of the 1850s personified the stylish, well-bred man-about-town, and Proust has left us an appealing description. "Edouard Manet was of medium height and physically very strong. There was a rhythm in the way he moved, added to which his particular rolling walk gave him a peculiar elegance. Even when he tried to exaggerate this rolling walk and assume the drawl of the Parisian street urchin, he could never succeed in being vulgar. One was always conscious of his breeding. His forehead was broad, his nose drawn in a bold straight line. His mouth, turned up at the corners, was mocking . . . Few men have been as attractive as he."

All his contemporaries agree that Manet was not only attractive but also immensely likable; he was reported as retaining his smile, "like a schoolboy in love," even in his final illness. And yet, as Renoir noticed, "the incomprehensible thing is that Manet, so gentle and affectionate, was always attacked, whereas Degas, so vitriolic, violent and uncompromising, was accepted by the Academy, the public and the revolutionaries." Discreetly generous financially to friends in need (he had some private means), Manet also appears to have done the decent thing by his Dutch mistress Suzanne Leenhoff. She had been brought into the Manet household to give piano lessons, and the young Edouard, only a year or two her junior, had begun a liaison with her. In 1852 she bore a child, whom she named Léon-Edouard, initially passing him off as her godson and later as her younger brother. It is generally assumed that he was Manet's son. His mother knew of the affair, though it was concealed from his father, and Manet married her in 1862, a year after his father's death.

EDOUARD MANET
The Old Musician
1862, National Gallery of Art, Washington

Manet was working on this painting at the same time as *Music in the Tuileries Gardens* (see page 17). The latter portrays the upper section of society, while this work depicts its poorer members, whom the new city developments were uprooting. The figures of Manet's own *Absinthe Drinker* and the barefoot girl carrying a baby, someone who inhabited the "Little Poland" area around Manet's studio, are combined with those of the Wandering Jew, the Old Musician, and Gilles the sad clown character, derived from Watteau, here protected by a dark twin.

EDOUARD MANET
The Dead Toreador
1863, National Gallery of Art, Washington

This painting is the center of a much larger canvas which Manet cut down for dramatic effect, isolating the single figure spread diagonally across the canvas. The influence of Velasquez is clearly apparent; this work may even have been inspired by a painting in the National Gallery, London, formerly attributed to the master. It depicts a dead soldier in an identical pose executed in the same coloring, tonal values, lighting and brushwork.

The influence of Spanish painting

In 1856 Manet left Couture's studio and travelled to visit various collections of great masters, journeying first to Holland, Germany, Prague and Austria and then to Italy. Although he did not reach Spain until ten years later, Spanish painting had formed a powerful influence on him since the start of his career, and his earliest biographer, Edmond Bazire, explains that although "his travels abroad were interrupted, he contented himself with daily visits to the Louvre. There he was deeply impressed by the Spaniards. As soon as he had become thoroughly acquainted with the works of Velasquez and Goya, fresh perspectives opened up before his eyes. After studying these pictures, where black becomes luminous, he began to show a new awareness of the quality of light, and from that moment, all his former research was upset . . . But Spain was nagging at him now, and suddenly he grasped it with both hands. Whilst respecting its art, he wished at the same time to rejuvenate it, and from ancient moulds he fashioned something new."

By 1867 over half of Manet's work was on a Spanish theme, and he was dubbed the "Spanish Parisian." Velasquez was the artist he admired above all others, and he singled out the Spanish master's *Little Cavaliers* (now thought to be by the painter's son-in-law, Mazo). "Ah! That's clean. How disgusted one is with these stews and gravies." What attracted him was the robust handling of color, the bold brushwork and the dramatic contrasts, so very different to the dead colors and smooth polish of the paintings admired by the Ecole des Beaux Arts.

The *Absinthe Drinker* of 1859 demonstrates his radical departure towards a new means of pictorial expression. The Spanish flavor is evident in the somber coloring, the lack of background detail and the use of black, while the foreground bottle is a direct echo of Velasquez, who often included still-life detail in both his portraits and his religious paintings. Manet showed the picture to his erstwhile master, and although Zola maintained that Couture's influence could be seen in the "studio technique," Couture himself was unimpressed. "The only drunkard is you," he said, a sneer which marked the end of their relationship.

EDOUARD MANET
The Absinthe Drinker
1858-59, Ny Carlsberg Glyptotek, Copenhagen

This painting was rejected by the Salon of 1859. The influence of Couture is evident in the treatment of the face, and the somber coloring echoes that of the Spanish masters. Manet himself explained that, "I have made a Parisian type, observed in Paris, while putting into execution the technical naïveté I found in the painting by Velasquez. They do not understand. Perhaps they will understand better if I make a Spanish type." He made no reference to the bizarre arrangement of the sitter's left leg and foot, which has invited much complex interpretation.

This was the first painting that Manet sent to the Salon, but like so many of his later works, it was rejected, being criticized for the very features that were to become the hallmarks of his art. The jury objected to the dramatic coloring, innovatory treatment of space and eccentric choice of subject, the "cult of systematic exaggeration," as one jury member put it. But although the subject certainly contrasted with those found acceptable at the Salon, it was completely in accord with Baudelaire's advocacy of a new kind of art depicting contemporary themes.

New concepts of space

Manet always longed to be accepted by the art establishment, and continued to submit works to the Salon, but he never achieved the kind of fame he envisaged. His painting *Music in the Tuileries* (see page 17) caused an uproar, as did the two subsequent works, *Déjeuner sur l'herbe* (see page 25) and *Olympia* (see page 29). In 1863 the Salon jury rejected over 4000 paintings, including all Manet's entries, and the indignation of the artists was so vociferous that Napoleon III ordered the rejected works to be displayed in the galleries adjoining those of the Palais d'Industrie, which housed the Salon. It became a popular amusement to visit the Salon des Refusés and laugh at the Manets, whose flatness, lack of modeling, "brutal beauty" and unusual treatment of space became the talk of the town.

Such was the impact of Manet's rejection of the theory of perspective, an aspect of art dogma that had been unquestioned for five centuries, that it will be useful to look briefly at its history in the context of his work. The discovery of mathematical perspective is credited to the 15th-century Florentine architect Brunelleschi. Based on the assumption that receding parallel lines appear to meet at a vanishing point on the horizon, he demonstrated the use of a grid system to create the illusion of figures and objects receding in space. No one is sure whether Manet's denial of this time-honored system was deliberate or simply an unconscious result of the personal vision which was never destroyed or weakened by academic training. His

EDOUARD MANET
The Execution of Maximilian
1868, Kunsthalle, Mannheim

Manet borrowed freely from Goya's *Third of May, 1808,* which he had seen two years earlier in Madrid. He was interested in the idea of commemorating on canvas an event of modern history, and had been affected by the execution of Maximilian, the Austrian archduke who had been installed as emperor of Mexico by Napoleon III. Manet worked on the subject for over a year, producing four oil paintings and a lithograph. This work, the latest, is the largest and most finished.

treatment of space has baffled generations of critics, who either bewail his "compositional difficulties" or view his radical departures as the result of two influences that were to alter the aesthetic idiom in the latter half of the century – photography and the Japanese print.

Photography questioned the whole notion of how we see. The camera, termed the "petrified Cyclops," records with one static eye instead of the two moving ones with which we actually view the world, giving a flattened and sometimes distorted image of reality which many artists found intriguing. Japanese prints, which started to come into the country in large numbers in the 19th century, and were avidly collected by artists and connoisseurs, offered a totally new concept of spatial arrangement. Figures were cropped, form was suggested by line

HIROSHIGE
Hisaka in the Sayo Mountains
1833-34

Manet was one of the earliest collectors of Japanese prints in Paris. The discovery of eastern art was a contributory factor in the revolution that challenged the dominance of the Western system of perspective in the second half of the 19th century. The flat, linear quality and absence of intermediate colors and tones, notable features of Japanese prints, are also evident in much of Manet's work.

EDOUARD MANET
Still life with Brioche
c1880, Private collection

Manet was particularly interested in still lifes at two separate periods, the first being from 1864-65 and the second at the end of his life. Before the mid-19th century, still life had not been considered a subject worthy of critical attention, but by the 1860s it had become popular. Manet's still lifes were not painted for the official Salon, but for picture dealers in return for modest payment, or for friends and acquaintances.

instead of tonal modeling, and perspective by means of overlapping shapes. Although Manet did not make direct use of Japanese idioms, as artists like Edgar Degas and James Whistler were to, the Eastern system of perspective must have appeared as a viable alternative to the Western one and provided encouragement to an artist who, whether consciously or unconsciously, was challenging the accepted rules.

The quest for official acceptance

By 1865 Manet was generally regarded as the leader of an ever-growing group of non-conformist artists. They were nicknamed "Manet's band," and would all meet on Friday evenings at the Café Guerbois on the Boulevard Clichy, where two tables were set aside for them. These were the painters who were to become the Impressionists, and they all acknowledged a debt to Manet, yet when he was asked to exhibit with them at the first Impressionist Exhibition of 1874 he refused. "Instead of huddling together in a separatist group," he said, "you should put on a tailcoat and go out into the world." This remark shows his essential conservatism; others might have seen him as a bohemian and anti-establishment revolutionary, but this is not how he saw himself. Even while painting works that he knew would not find favor in the official Salon he still sought success within it.

The importance of the Salon cannot be over emphasized – until later in the century it was the only art market place, and it was virtually impossible for an artist to succeed without its seal of approval. In 1867, however, having failed to gain official recognition, Manet staged a show of his own work in a temporary building on the Place de l'Alma. Crowds arrived to laugh at the fifty paintings on show, but notice was beginning to be taken of him: a year later Zola maintained that his reputation was assured, and Degas jokingly told him he was "as famous as Garibaldi."

By 1870 he had ceased to be vilified, and by the 1880s works by other artists which showed his influence were also acceptable. Tragically, before he could develop into maturity, he was attacked by the debilitating disease locomotor ataxia, which caused his premature death at the age of fifty-one, ten days after the amputation of his left leg. But eighteen months before his death he had received the accolade coveted by every Frenchman who craves recognition – he was made a Chevalier of the Légion d'Honneur.

Manet's Painting Methods

This detail from *Olympia* shows Manet's use of full-on lighting, giving strong contrasts of light and shade and no half-tones.

Detail from *Déjeuner sur l'herbe.* Manet's early paintings show the influence of Velasquez, whom he admired for his use of deep, rich blacks.

This detail from *Music in the Tuileries Gardens* shows Manet's use of bold brushwork and the wet-in-wet technique.

Manet developed his personal style early in his career, while still a student, using a slurred, wet-in-wet technique of mixing the colors directly on the canvas. The paintings admired by the art establishment of the day were highly finished, built up gradually in successive layers over a tonal foundation, with the color added last and the brushwork virtually invisible. Manet, in contrast, used only a single skin (or coat) of paint and suppressed middle tones to emphasize bold areas of light and dark. He liked a strong, direct light source, which helped to eliminate half-tones and created flattened planes of light and shade; his paintings were criticized for their harsh, flat appearance and lack of modeling.

One of the academic theories of the day was that bright colors should never be placed side by side without gradual transitions to blend one into another, but Manet boldly juxtaposed clear colors such as bright greens and acid yellows, exploiting pale grounds for their luminosity and flatness – also in direct contrast to academic practice. It is more difficult to create an illusion of depth on a pale ground than a dark one, and he used this to advantage to create a shallow pictorial space.

Surprisingly, Manet worked slowly and hesitantly. Monet said of his *Olympia* (see page 29) that "he had a laborious, careful method. He always wanted his paintings to have the air of being painted at a single sitting; but often . . . would scrape down what he had executed during the day. He kept only the lowest layer, which had great charm and finesse, on which he would begin improvising."

Manet's palette probably comprised lead (1) and zinc whites, black (2), raw umber (3), yellow ochre (4), red earth (5) or red lead, ultramarine blue (6), cobalt blue (7), viridian green (8), possibly cobalt green (9) and chrome (10) green.

In the 1860s, when he painted *Music in the Tuileries Gardens* Manet's palette probably comprised the following colors, with the addition of lead and zinc whites. 1 black; 2 raw umber; 3 yellow ocher; 4 red earth or red lead; 5 ultramarine blue; 6 cobalt blue; 7 viridian; 8 (possibly) cobalt green; 9 chrome green.

CHRONOLGY OF MANET'S LIFE

1832 Born in Paris, eldest of three brothers.
1839 Starts school in Vaugirard, then a suburb of Paris.
1842 Enters the Collège Rollin, where he meets life-long friend Antonin Proust. Takes course in drawing.
1848 December: joins navy and sails to Rio de Janeiro. Spends time drawing.
1849 July: Re-takes naval exams, but fails. Manages to convince father to allow him to study art.
1850 Enters the studio of Thomas Couture. Also attends the Académie Suisse in the evenings.
1852 Birth of a son to Suzanne Leenhoff, piano teacher to the Manet brothers, and Manet's future wife. The child is believed to have been his.
1853 Visits Italy, and makes copies of the old masters.
1856 Leaves Couture's studio, and travels widely, visiting various European collections of paintings in Belgium, Holland, Germany, Austria and Italy.
1859 Submits *The Absinthe Drinker* to the Salon jury, but it is rejected.
1861 *The Guitar Player* received with acclaim at the Salon. Manet meets Degas in the Louvre. The Galerie Martinet in the Boulevard des Italiens begins to show his paintings.
1862 Death of Manet's father.
1863 *Déjeuner sur l'herbe* rejected by the official Salon and shown at the Salon des Refusés, where it creates scandal. October 28, to Holland; marries Suzanne Leenhoff.
1865 *Olympia* shown at the Salon causes an uproar. Manet leaves for Spain.
1866 Zola publishes an article on Manet, singling him out as the greatest modern master.

Lola de Valence

The Seine Banks at Argenteuil

Girl Serving Beer

1867 Manet stages private exhibition of his most important paintings in a temporary building on the Place d'Alma. Meets Monet and Berthe Morisot, later to become his sister-in-law.
1868 Visits England briefly. Works with Berthe Morisot.
1870 July 19: outbreak of the Franco-Prussian war. Serves with Degas in the artillery of the National Guard during the Siege of Paris.
1871 February: war ends, Manet leaves Paris to join his family in Bordeaux.
1872 The dealer Durand-Ruel buys about thirty of his paintings. Spends summer in Holland. Dutch influence apparent in painting *Le Bon Bock,* greeted with approval at the Salon the following year.
1873 Beginning of friendship with the poet Stéphane Mallarmé.
1874 Declines to exhibit at the first Impressionist Exhibition. Spends Summer with Monet and Renoir at Argenteuil.
1875 September: makes trip to Venice.
1879 First symptoms of locomotor ataxia.
1881 Wins a second-class medal for a portrait, and is therefore entitled to exhibit at the Salon without submitting his work to the jury. Becomes very ill. His schoolfriend Antonin Proust, now Minister of Arts, secures for him the Légion d'Honneur, though the President of the Republic refuses to sign his confirmation.
1882 *Bar at the Folies-Bergère* well received at the Salon.
1883 April 20: bedridden, Manet's left leg is amputated to halt gangrene. Ten days later he dies.

THE PAINTINGS

Music in the Tuileries Gardens

1860

30×46¾in/76×119cm

Oil on canvas

National Gallery, London

This painting is an informal record of the artist's literary, artistic and musical friends enjoying an afternoon concert in the Tuileries Gardens in Paris. Working from both photographs and sketches of the group of well-to-do Parisians at leisure, Manet has given us a slice of contemporary life devoid of the heroic or dramatic content fashionable with the art establishment of the time. His friendship with the poet and occasional art critic Charles Baudelaire must certainly have influenced his development as the painter of modern life, although it seems that as a youth he had already exhibited signs of an interest in a new pictorial expression based on everyday subjects. Proust was later to comment on this, telling us how Manet reacted scathingly to Diderot's comments that the painting of contemporary dress would perforce render a picture old-fashioned, "How imbecilic," said Manet. "One must be of one's time, paint what one sees,without worrying about fashion." Baudelaire, Manet's constant companion during the early 1860s, had expounded his views on modern painting in *The Heroism of Modern Life* (1846). Here he maintained that "we have only to open our eyes to discover our own heroism." The French salon regarded contemporary life as too trivial a subject for painting.

It is hard for the modern audience to appreciate the anger this painting aroused; one visitor even threatened to attack it with his walking stick. It was not only that the subject matter was unusual and accorded ill with the Salon visitors' expectations; the technique was shocking too. Paintings chosen by the Salon jury always had a high degree of "finish," and Manet's lack of polish and bold brushwork, although virtues for the modern viewer, must have seemed slapdash and even impertinent. We see it as possibly the first modern picture, but the gallery-going public, from the mid-1860s on, took great pleasure in deriding Manet's work.

Having trained for six years in the studio of Thomas Couture, Manet had both received and practiced traditional lessons of academic painting. Couture advocated the method of building up a painting in successive thin layers, unifying tone and color by scumbling white pigment over a darker ground, or applying colored glazes over the painted surface. Manet soon discarded this technique in favor of a simpler, more direct application of pigment to create a more spontaneous effect. He did not always achieve this at the first attempt: visitors to his studio were surprised to see the way he "attacked" the canvas, often scraping off the image many times without dirtying the subsequent overpainting or diminishing the impression of spontaneity.

There is evidence to suggest that Manet intended to work further on this painting. A. C. Hanson in *Manet and The Modern Tradition* points out how the center of the picture (which would usually be the most detailed and carefully worked) is the part most loosely painted, and that while some portraits are clearly indentifiable, other figures seem to be waiting for the addition of significant features. "The paint itself," she observes, "is extremely thin in many areas and there is evidence of scraping as though in preparation for further layers of paint. The build-up of rich color relationships seems not to have yet taken place." The date of the painting is in a different color from the signature, which implies that it was probably not signed until just before it was shown in the Galerie Martinet in 1863. If it was only a partially finished sketch, Manet may have exhibited it to demonstrate an attempt "to capture the raw beauty and vivid reality of his own society."

The use of a thinned light brown, evident in certain areas of the canvas, shows that Manet worked in a traditional way, creating an *ébauche*, or monochrome underpainting, before laying in color. The semi-transparency of the greenery in the upper half of the painting shows evidence of scraping, and reveals the white of the underlying primed canvas. The unfinished character of the picture, which is little more than an oil sketch, contributes to its vitality. But the apparent naturalism is misleading, for the way the figures are shown, looking outward as though to involve the viewer in the scene, was a device Manet was to develop in much of his later work. In contrast to the density of the crowd that occupies the central horizontal band, the area immediately at the foreground is unoccupied, allowing the foreground figures to stand out clear and unobscured.

1

2

1 The figures in the crowd are all portrait studies of the artist's friends. On the extreme left is Manet himself, standing next to Albert de Balleroy, the animal painter with whom he shared a studio. Seated is Zacharie Astruc, the journalist whose lines were inscribed on the frame of *Olympia* (see page 29). The mustachioed figure immediately behind him may well be that of the journalist Aurélien Scholl, the epitome of the young dandy. Between Manet and de Balleroy can be glimpsed the head of the writer Champfleury, for whose *Cats* Manet produced an illustration and poster.

2 This central foreground detail offers a charming vignette of two very young girls playing on the ground with buckets and spades, and provides a small central focus of activity in a setting of enforced leisure. Their white dresses and huge sashes tied in big bows create the kind of bold dash of detail that Manet was to further develop in his Spanish-style works.

3 *Actual size detail* The veiled seated figure is most probably that of Madame Loubens. The brushwork is loose and free, with the strokes following the direction of the flowing folds of the dress. The artist has worked quickly, with a loaded brush, leaving small areas of bare canvas uncovered in places. The gray-blues of the veil were produced by dabs and streaks of black, painted wet-in-wet.

3 *Actual size detail*

Lola de Valence

1862
$48\frac{3}{8} \times 36\frac{1}{4}$in/123×92cm
Oil on canvas
Musée d'Orsay, Paris

Lola de Valence was the star ballerina of a Spanish dance troupe which performed to great acclaim at the Paris Hippodrome between August and November of 1862. Manet's portrait reveals two important sources of inspiration. The first is Goya: Lola's pose is almost identical to that of the *Duchess of Albi* in Goya's portrait. Initially the background, like Goya's, was neutral, but apparently Manet followed the advice of friends and inserted an appropriate backdrop in 1867. The second influence is Daumier, whose comic lithograph "A queen preparing for a great soliloquy" was the inspiration for the behind-scenes stage setting. Later, as X-ray examinations show, Manet extended the painting above and below by about 4in (10cm).

In painting a Spanish dancer on stage, Manet was continuing a well-established Parisian tradition, yet the vigor of the brushwork and color mark it as a new kind of work. Attracted by the exoticism of the troupe, he received permission to paint them on the three days of the week when there were no performances. Beginning with rough sketches and drawings, he then painted the ballet scenes from life. Spanish themes were increasingly dominating Manet's work, and by 1867 over half of his fifty-three oils exhibited were of Spanish themes. The vogue for things Spanish had reached a highpoint in the 1830s, receiving a further stimulus with the marriage of Napoleon III to a young Spanish beauty, Eugénie de Montijo, in 1853. Lola herself was intriguing and exciting to Manet and his circle, some of whom were wont to pen sonnets and serenades to her charms. Baudelaire described her as possessing a "beauty of a type both mysterious and playful at the same time." After seeing the painting in Manet's studio he composed a quatrain on the work, which he hoped to have inscribed on the canvas. It is translated as follows:

My friends, I know the desire to range among
The beauties that surround us; but the charm
Of Lola de Valence does all disarm
The unexpected charm of a rose and black jewel.

"This mysterious rose and black jewel," wrote the poet Paul Valéry, "seems to me to be less suitable for the solid and robust dancer, who, weighed down with a rich and heavy skirt, but sure of the suppleness of her muscles, waits proudly in the shadow of the wings for the signal to leap forth into the irregular movement of her frenzied dance, than for the cold nude *Olympia*."

In fact the dominant colors in the painting are not rose and black, but orange, yellow and green on black. The colorful costume of the dancer is set off by the monochrome backdrop of the reverse side of the stage scenery, beyond which we glimpse the back of a performer and the audience. Zola noted that "the painter by now is already working only in masses, and his Spanish woman is painted largely in bold contrasts. The whole canvas is painted in only two tones." The painting's reception among the critics when exhibited in 1863 was considerably less rapturous than that of Manet's friends, who considered it a great success. Doubtless the lack of "finish" was regretted as usual, as was the juxtaposition of bright colors without mediating half-tones. Paul Manz, the Director General of the Ministry of Fine Arts, commented on the artist's "generous, fertile vigor" but did not approve "the medley of red, blue and yellow which is a caricature of color rather than color itself," concluding that, "It may be a very faithful kind of art, but it is not sound."

Manet's interest in things Spanish is evident here both in the subject and in the pose, which derives from Goya's portrait of the *Duchess of Albi.* Manet originally painted the Andalusian dancer against a neutral background, which would have made the impact of the strong, bold color contrasts even greater, but he later changed this on the advice of friends. Initially a formal portrait of the dancer holding a balletic pose, the addition of stage scenery adds an anecdotal dimension, creating the impression that the artist is backstage, catching the obliging performer on canvas just before she goes on stage. The vitality of the color was noted and praised by contemporary critics, but the painting was criticized for its lack of subtle modulations.

1

2

1 Manet was much attracted to this Spanish beauty, finding the contrasts of her coloring – raven hair and pale complexion – well suited to the dramatic style of his early years. He has chosen a flattering three-quarter view to show her enigmatic half smile to advantage, and has emphasized the blackness of her hair by the white shawl above her head.

2 Although Manet's approach to his work was always painterly, he nevertheless greatly admired the work of the great draughtsman Ingres, whose *Madame Montessier* may have been inspirational in this portrait. The jeweled right arm is particularly reminiscent of Ingres, and the lessons Manet absorbed from his first teacher Couture are also evident in the use of a misty overlay of semi-transparent white pigment to convey the impression of Lola's white lace shawl.

3 *Actual size detail* The "riot of red, blue, yellow and black" which the contemporary critic Paul Manz described as a "caricature of color" is clearly evident in this detail. The large flowers are realized with a few bold dashes of pigment, and the tassel of the dancer's fan is created with a sweep of blue into which white has been streaked.

3 *Actual size detail*

DEJEUNER SUR L'HERBE

(The Picnic)
1863
81¾ × 104in/208 × 264.5cm
Oil on canvas
Musée d'Orsay, Paris

"This nude has shocked the public, which has been unable to see anything but her in the picture. Good Heavens! How indecent! What! A woman without a stitch of clothing seated between two fully clad men! Such a thing has never been seen before! But this belief is gross error; in the Musée du Louvre there are more than fifty pictures in which clothed people mix with the naked. But no one goes to the Louvre to be shocked." These words are taken from Emile Zola's article entitled *A New Way of Painting: Edouard Manet,* in which he championed the painter's work.

"It was considered," Zola continued, "that the artist's choice of subject was obscene and showy, whereas all the artist had sought to do was to obtain an effect of strong contrasts and bold masses." But Manet, while grateful for the praise from an influential young writer, would not have been happy with the assessment of his work as an arrangement of colored shapes. He refused Zola's offer to write the catalog to his private exhibition, giving the polite excuse that such fulsome praise would seem immodest. But what Manet actually felt was that he had been misunderstood. "Already many people speak well of me," he said, "but I feel they don't understand me. They don't grasp what there is in me or at least what I try to show."

Zola described this painting solely in formal terms. "What you have to look for in the painting is not just a picnic on the grass, but the whole landscape, with its bold and subtle passages, its broadly painted, solid foreground, its light and delicate background and that firm flesh modeled in broad areas of light, those supple and strong materials, and, particularly that splash of white among the green leaves in the background . . ." Zola makes no reference to traditional sources of inspiration for the painting, but Antonin Proust maintained in his memoirs that Manet's initial source was Giorgione's *Concert Champêtre* in the Louvre (possibly completed by Titian). He recorded how he and Manet were strolling along the banks of the Seine at Argenteuil discussing their work. "It seems that I've got to paint a nude," declared Manet. "Very well! I'll do 'em one . . . I copied a picture of some women by Giorgione — the women with the musicians — but it's too black . . . I would like to redo it and make it translucent, using models like those people we see over there."

Feeling that a nude was expected of him, Manet chose to reinterpret a classical theme in a modern idiom. Giorgione's depiction of an Arcadian idyll, which is further developed in Titian's *Sacred and Profane Love,* may have provided Manet's original theme and the oblique allegory, but the iconography derives directly from an engraving by Marcantonio Raimondi of Raphael's *Judgement of Paris* (opposite below).

In spite of its outdoor setting, the picture is very obviously a studio work, and shows a self-conscious anti-naturalism both in the lack of modeling, especially evident in the girl's flesh, and the strange rendition of space. There is little traditional perspective: the figure of the bather, behind the main group, is out of scale, and the background is reminiscent of a stage backdrop, which implies recession while simultaneously showing an obvious lack of it. The flash-lit effect, flattering the forms and eliminating half-tones, suggests that photography may have been influential in its conception, as was probably Manet's familiarity with Japanese prints, which emphasize contour and pattern and use no tonal modeling. Both these art forms sustained Manet's assertion that "light appeared to the human eye with a unity such that a single tone was sufficient to render it, moreover it was preferable, crude though it might seem, to pass suddenly from light to darkness rather than accumulate features the eye does not see."

The subject matter, while no longer arousing the hostility it did in Manet's lifetime, is still enigmatic. It is seen by some as a symbolic landscape in which dualities of town and country, male and female, past and present, purity and sensuality are alluded to. Manet's close friend Antonin Proust suggested that the original inspiration came when Manet saw some bathers in the Seine, and said he would like to paint them, but this claim may have been the result of Proust's desire to assert his friend's status as one of the forerunners of outdoor painting. Manet revealed almost nothing of his reasons for experimenting with new ways of depicting form and space, claiming that "I only paint what I see in front of me, with sincerity."

MARCANTONIO RAIMONDI
The Judgement of Paris
(detail) after Raphael
British Museum, London

1

2

1 According to Antonin Proust, both Manet's brothers — Eugène and Gustave — posed in turn for this figure. The tasseled cap worn by students at the time contributes to the flavor of a bohemian picnic, a modern equivalent of a *fête champêtre*, which offended contemporary critics. The heavy use of black in the cap, hair, beard and coat, striking against the light, even color of the face, contrasts strongly with the paler tones of the boat behind.

2 The selection of foodstuffs essential to a picnic lunch provided Manet with the opportunity of composing a luscious still life at the lower left of the canvas. The fact that the assemblage of ripe fruit is unrealistic — June cherries with September figs — suggests that there may be a symbolic element, possibly relating to the naked woman on whose discarded dress the picnic lies. The silver flask at the right enhances the sense of luxury and liberality, another cause for complaint among the critics.

3 *Actual size detail* The pose of this semi-clad wading figure may derive from that of St John in Raphael's tapestry cartoon of *The Miraculous Draught of Fishes.* Out of proportion in spatial terms, she occupies a space which was traditionally placed in the middle distance. Here she looks as though she inhabits the lower half of a backdrop to a stage set.

3 *Actual size detail*

Olympia

1863

$51\frac{3}{8} \times 74\frac{3}{4}$ in / 130.5×190 cm

Oil on canvas

Musée d'Orsay, Paris

The year of 1863 was an important one for Manet. He married his mistress of eleven years, Suzanne Leenhoff, and painted what are probably his two most famous works, *Déjeuner sur l'herbe* (see page 25) and this painting. *Olympia*, however, was not exhibited until two years later, in spite of the encouragement provided by Manet's close friends, as he was reluctant to invite a repeat of the scandal that had followed the showing of the *Déjeuner*. But Baudelaire continued to press him to exhibit the nude, and it was duly submitted to the Salon of 1865.

Its critical reception confirmed Manet's misgivings. It was condemned as an outrage to public morality. "Nothing so cynical has ever been seen as this *Olympia*," wrote the critic of *Le Grand Journal*. ". . . A sort of female gorilla, an india-rubber deformity, surrounded by black, lying on a bed, completely nude . . . Her hand is clenched in a sort of indecent contraction. Truly women about to become mothers, and young maidens, would do well, if they were prudent, to run away from this spectacle." It was Manet's detachment, reflected in the cool gaze of his model, that shocked people. This nude is very different from the titillating variety, such as Cabanel's *Birth of Venus* (see page 6), which received high acclaim. It is an unsentimental and not particularly graceful portrayal of a young prostitute, looking out at us as though summing up the next client. The hissing cat, its back arched, indicates the arrival of a third party — the spectator — unseen beyond the confines of the frame. The black maidservant, a character who traditionally appears as companion-procuress of such women, emphasizes the nature of the subject's profession, as does the bouquet of wrapped flowers she is offering, presumably just received from a gentleman who has enjoyed her favors.

Zola expressed to Manet the main objection to the painting. "She has the serious fault of resembling young ladies of your acquaintance. Isn't that so?" This nude, while deriving in pose from classical Venuses, is not looking wistfully away or feigning sleep. No modest blush rises to her cheek, and the gesture of the hand, unlike that in Titian's *Venus of Urbino* (opposite below), was seen as a means of drawing attention to her sex rather than concealing it. Manet was disappointed that none of the critics mentioned his use of traditional references, although the painting clearly derives from Titian's masterpiece, with an amusing inversion in the exchange of the lapdog, a symbol of fidelity, for the cat, associated with lasciviousness.

The model was Victorine Meurent, who also posed for *Déjeuner*. Slight and elegant, Manet had picked her out in a crowd, and she became his favorite model for some ten years. In the 1860s, slenderness was the vogue for female beauty, and Baudelaire explained the attraction of the currently typical *femme fatale* by saying that "there is in thinness an indecency which makes it charming . . . Thinness is more bare, more indecent than fatness." Mallarmé saw *Olympia* as a "wan and wasted courtesan, showing to the public for the first time the non-traditional, unconventional nude . . . captivating and repulsive at the same time, eccentric and new." She is posed awkwardly on her silken cushions, and the stiffness of her upper torso has nothing of the voluptuous relaxation of Goya's *Naked Maja*. This may have been a further inspiration for the work, while the oriental shawl associates it with the Odalisques of Ingres. Ironically, although at the time the public would have disclaimed any connection with the revered master, when *Olympia* became a modern icon and was placed in the Louvre, she was hung next to an Ingres nude. An observer remarked how strange it was that after all that fuss the difference between the two was barely discernible.

Painted largely in monochrome planes of even color, light in the foreground and dark in the background, the picture is enlivened by touches of polychrome detail. The contrast between foreground and background is accentuated by the silhouette of the figure, which divides the painting into two halves, the lower one stressing the horizontal and the upper one the vertical. Just as Titian's *Venus of Urbino* (left) was the model for Manet's painting, *Olympia* itself became an icon for subsequent painters. Faithfully copied by Gauguin and interpreted more freely by Cézanne, it has also been affectionately parodied by artists as diverse as Picasso, Dubuffet and Larry Rivers. Strangely, although the painting is imbued with the spirit of Baudelaire's poetry, the words inscribed on the frame are those of an inferior poet, Zacharie Astruc. Perhaps Manet felt he owed a debt of gratitude to Astruc, who had defended his work in 1863.

TITIAN
Venus of Urbino
1538, Uffizi Gallery, Florence

1

2

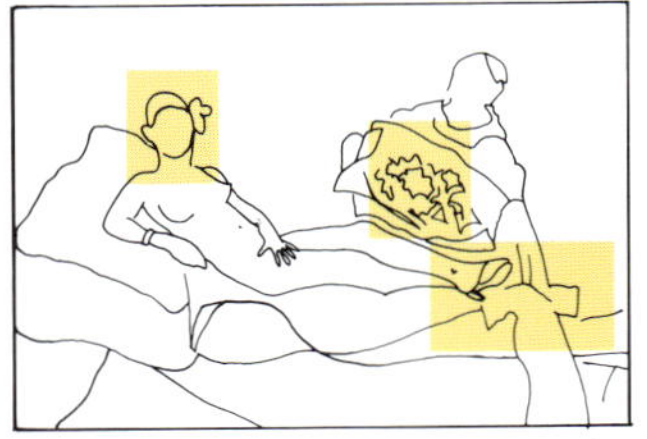

1 Like the bloom in her hair, the pearl earrings and black velvet choker emphasize Olympia's nakedness. The head, with its cool gaze trained on the spectator, is scarcely modeled, although a light, semi-transparent brown has been used to trace the model's pointed chin. Contemporary critics regretted the way the artist had upset traditional values, "esteeming a head no more highly than a shoe, and assigning more importance to a bunch of flowers than to the face of a woman."

2 Like the oriental shawl, which discloses rather than conceals, the slippers accentuate the artificiality of the figure. The colors in the floral bouquet are echoed in the blue trim on the slippers and the red and green of the embroidered flowers.

3 *Actual size detail* The bouquet, which provides a counterbalance to Olympia's head, is composed of a central large white flower immediately surrounded by alternating dashes of light blue and dark green. These are encircled by touches of white, offset by four evenly spaced red accents. Sprays of fern, painted wet-in-wet, encompass the bouquet. By way of contrast to the thin application of colored pigment on some of the flowers, the wrapping paper has been created with a bold sweep of thick white paint, which in places overlaps the foliage.

3 *Actual size detail*

The Balcony

1868
67×49in/170×124.5cm
Oil on canvas
Musée d'Orsay, Paris

The ambiguity of this painting puzzled contemporary critics. "One doesn't quite know," wrote Paul Manz in the *Gazette des Beaux-Arts,* "what these good people are doing on the balcony, and the German critics, curious about the philosophical meaning of things, would be very hard put to understand or explain the content.".

Inspired by Goya's *Majas on the Balcony,* Manet has replaced the drama and mystery of the Spanish work with a modern image of a trio of people seemingly frozen in their separateness, perhaps reflecting the social fragmentation of modern city life. It has been suggested of this enigmatic painting that it is an allegorical work relating to the artist's sources of inspiration — Spain on the left, Japan on the right, and Dutch painting in the center. This could be so, but the painting seems to invite a psychological interpretation. The figures are tightly grouped yet seem to have no connection with one another, and the elusive quality of the picture is compounded by the shadowy figure of the boy bearing a tray in the background. The three people are the Impressionist painter Berthe Morisot (seated), the violinist Fanny Claus, and the landscape painter Antoine Guillemot. The figure of Berthe Morisot, who was to become Manet's sister-in-law, is the most arresting figure in the canvas. She wrote to her sister Edma, "I am more strange than ugly. It seems the epithet of *femme fatale* has been circulating among the curious." Fanny Claus is less powerfully realized. One of four highly talented musical sisters who played professionally as the Sainte-Cécile quartet, she also occasionally gave private recitals at Manet's house, to the piano accompaniment of Suzanne Manet. With her parasol in the crook of her arm, she is adjusting her gloves as though preparing to go out. Like Berthe, she looks out from the painting, not, we feel, at anything of interest in the street below, but in pensive reflection. Her face, which recalls the flat expressionlessness of a Japanese mask, seems to show evidence of Manet's practice of scraping off the painted surface before reworking. In a letter to Edma, their mother mentions the arduous hours of posing required by the painter. "Antoine says that he made him pose fifteen times to no effect and that Mademoiselle Claus is atrocious. But both of them, tired of posing on their feet, say to him, 'It's perfect — there is nothing more to be done over'. "

Berthe Morisot, in a letter to her sister, gives some idea of Manet's agitation during the exhibition of the painting. "I met Manet, looking very harassed. He begged me to go and see his picture because he himself didn't dare. I've never seen anybody with such an expressive face. He was laughing nervously, insisting one minute that his picture (*The Balcony*) was very bad and the next that it would be a great success."

The geometric structure of the composition, which stresses vertical lines — in the flanking shutters and the wrought-iron balustrade — suggests that Manet may have used the classical Golden Section to produce the most satisfying relationship of proportions, and he has certainly used the Renaissance pyrmidal form to contain the three figures. He has also attempted to create a new kind of spatial recession where, although a degree of three-dimensionality is suggested, we are constantly made aware of the flat surface of the canvas, a feature which was to become of paramount importance in modern art. His paintings were often criticized for their flatness, and here he has used no half-tones to give his forms conventional modelling, but instead has thrown the brightly lit frontal plane into stark contrast against the dark background. There is little color; the painting is almost a Whistlerian symphony in green and white balanced by a central passage of darkness and offset by touches of blue.

The reviewer Jules-Antoine Castagnary was one of those to be bewildered by this painting. "On the balcony I see two women, one of whom is very young. Are they sisters? Is this a mother and daughter? I don't know. And then one has seated herself apparently just to enjoy the view of the street; the other is putting on her gloves as if she were about to leave. This contradictory attitude baffles me . . ." It is precisely this enigmatic quality which has made the picture one of the most powerful images of late 19th-century French painting. In 1950 its status as a "late Old Master" work was acknowledged pictorially by the Surrealist painter René Magritte in his *Perspective: the Balcony by Manet.* Magritte represented the three figures as coffins in an identical setting, symbolizing the desire to "kill off the Old Masters."

1

2

2 The dog playing with the ball provides a spot of animation in the static composition. The flowered ceramic container which holds the potted hydrangea offers the artist the possibility of displaying to full effect his proficiency in rendering the effects of a light-reflective surface.

1 The model for this shadowy figure was, by his own admission, Léon Leenhoff, Manet's godson and probably also his natural son. The motif of the young boy carrying a vessel appears in an earlier work of Manet's, a copy of *The Spanish Cavaliers*, then attributed to Velasquez. The indistinctness of execution, in contrast to the other figures, suggests a degree of spatial recession in a work which is otherwise deliberately flattened, almost two-dimensional.

3 *Actual size detail* This is one of Manet's finest portraits of the Impressionist painter Berthe Morisot, a friend and later sister-in-law of Manet. He was attracted by her quiet reserve and dramatic, dark good looks, and painted her frequently. He also respected her work as a painter although he was wont jokingly to make light of her talent, remarking of her and her sister Edma that "The Mademoiselles Morisot are charming. Too bad they're not men. All the same, women as they are, they could serve the cause of painting by each marrying an academician, and bringing discord into the camp of the enemy." Berthe herself said that Manet's paintings "always makes me think of wild fruit, perhaps a little raw, but they far from displease me."

3 *Actual size detail*

Portrait of Emile Zola

1867-68

$57^1/_2 \times 44^3/_4$in/146×114cm

Oil on canvas

Musée d'Orsay, Paris

Grateful for the support of the young Zola, who had defended the *Déjeuner sur l'herbe,* (see page 25). Manet contacted him and offered to paint his portrait. Zola discussed sitting for this portrait in an article published on May 10, in *L'Evénement Illustré.* "The public is becoming used to Manet's work; the critics are calming down and have agreed to open their eyes; success is on its way . . . Manet's originality, which had once seemed prodigiously comic, now occasions them no more astonishment than that experienced by a child confronted by an unknown spectacle . . . When they see the name Manet they try to force a laugh . . . They go away, ill at ease, not knowing any more what to think; moved, in spite of themselves by the sincerity of his talent, prepared to admire it *next* year.

"From my point of view the success of Manet is assured. I never dared dream that it would be so rapid and deserving. It is singularly difficult to make the shrewdest people in the world admit a mistake. In France, a man whom ignorance has made a figure of fun is often condemned to live and die a figure of fun . . . there will still be jokes at the expense of the painter of *Olympia.* But from now on intelligent people have been won over, and as a result the mob will follow.

"From time to time, as I posed, half-asleep, I looked at the artist standing at his easel, with features drawn, clear-eyed, engrossed in his work. He had forgotten me, he no longer knew I was there, he simply copied me, as if I were some human beast, with a concentration and artistic integrity that I have seen nowhere else. And then I thought of the slovenly dauber of legend, of this Manet who was a figment of the imagination of caricaturists, who painted cats as a leg-pull.

"What, personally, astonished me, was the extreme conscientiousness of the artist. Often, when he was coping with a detail of secondary importance, I wanted to stop posing and give him the bad advice that he should 'make it up.' 'No,' he answered me, 'I can do nothing without nature. I do not know how to invent . . . If I am worth something today, it is due to exact interpretation and faithful analysis.'

"There lies all his talent. Before anything else, he is a naturalist. His eye sees and renders objects with elegant simplicity. I know I won't be able to make the blind like his pictures; but real artists will understand me when I speak of the slightly bitter charm of his works. The color of it is intense and extremely harmonious. And this, mark you, is the picture by a man who is accused of being able neither to paint nor draw."

This portrait broke new ground. It is an informal portrayal of the writer viewed from the side, in a study which contains references to both sitter and artist. On the wall a frame displays three pictures which hold special significance for Manet himself. Most prominent is a monochrome version of *Olympia* (see page 29), the most notorious work in the painter's *oeuvre.* In this version, a lock of hair falls over the nude's brow, and her head is turned to the writer as though in recognition of his praise for her and her creator. Above this can be seen the upper half of Velasquez's *Drinkers,* to which Manet had first been introduced by means of the copy shown here, and then seen in the original at the Prado when he visited Spain in 1865. To the left is a print of a wrestler by the Japanese artist Kuniaki II, an eastern contemporary of Manet. Manet was one of the earliest collectors of Japanese art in Paris. Directly below the framed display, amid the pamphlets on the desk, is Zola's article on Manet, and it is possible that the open book — which the sitter is holding but not reading — is Charles Blanc's *History of the Painters,* a work frequently consulted by the artist.

Manet's portrait of the young Zola corresponds closely to the novelist's own description of himself in his novel *L'Oeuvre,* in which he appears under the name of Sandoz. "Dark complexion, heavy set but not fat — at first. Head round and obstinate. chin square, nose square. Eyes soft in mask of energy. Neckpiece of black beard." The erect L-shape of the pose, and the distant, unengaged look of the sitter were remarked upon by contemporary viewers. The critic Jules-Antoine Castagnary praised the portrait as one of the best at the Salon of that year but regretted that "the face lacks modeling, and looks like a profile pasted onto a background," adding that Manet "sees black and white, and only with difficulty gets objects in the round." In fact, X-rays reveal initial modeling of the face which was subsequently deliberately overlaid, so clearly the flattening effect was intentional.

1

2

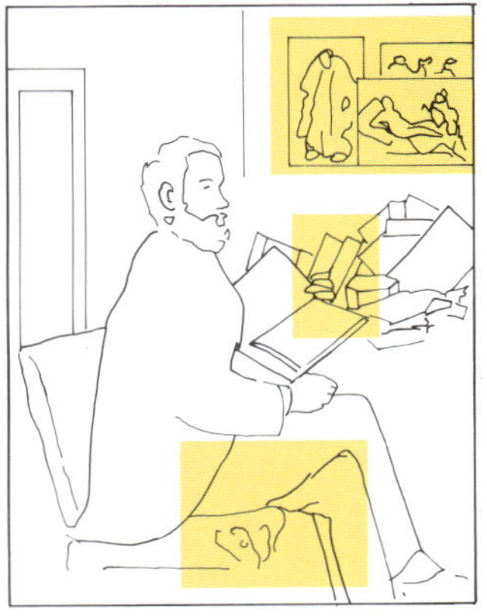

1 Degas had included a framed collection of prints in his picture *The Collector of Prints* painted the previous year. Here the three identifiable works, including Manet's own *Olympia*, are included for their importance for the artist rather than the sitter, although the position of Olympia's head, turned towards Zola, may suggest a mute gratitude for his defence of the painting. The juxtaposition of the Japanese print with the painting reveals the influence of Eastern art: in both works there is a dominant, flattened image whose silhouette is darkly outlined against paler tones. In the original print the robe was blue, but Manet altered the color to brown to harmonize with his gold and black color scheme.

2 The lower section of the canvas is much the most freely painted. While this treatment is admirably suited for suggesting the pattern and texture of the chair, certain contemporary reviewers criticized the artist for his neglect in not faithfully recreating the texture of the trousers.

3 *Actual size detail* Zola himself drew particular attention to the depiction of the hands in this work, remarking, "In short, here is skin, but real skin, without ridiculous *trompe l'oeil . . .*" When the painting was shown at the Salon, it met with a mixed reception, but the collection of books and objects cluttering the wall and table were admired as "astonishingly real."

3 *Actual size detail*

The Seine Banks at Argenteuil

1874

24×39¾in/61×101cm

Oil on canvas

National Gallery, London

During the summer of 1874, Manet worked closely with Monet and Renoir, the two arch-exponents of Impressionism, painting on the banks of the Seine. His family had a house at Gennevilliers, on the south bank, while Monet then lived at Argenteuil on the opposite side. The area is now an industrial suburb, but in Manet's day Argenteuil was a riverside retreat of country resorts and cottage gardens. Monet had settled there in 1871, and the place became popular with the Impressionist painters throughout the decade. It was close enough to Paris to allow visits to exhibitions, social gatherings and artist's suppliers, while simultaneously offering a range of landscape subjects, particularly the river. Although principally attracted to the pleasures of the city, Manet also delighted in working outdoors directly from nature. He had spent holidays at Argenteuil from childhood, and it is much in the holiday spirit that he approached the outdoor scenes painted at this time.

Manet's association with Monet led to a change in his work, but it was very much a cross-fertilization, with each artist learning from the other at different times. Some years earlier, when Monet had shown his *Camille,* a portrait of his wife-to-be, at the Salon of 1867, critics had noted the influence of Manet. This gave rise to André Gill's jest: "Monet or Manet? Monet. But we owe this Monet to Manet. Well done Monet. Thank you Manet." Seven years later the names could easily be inverted.

Manet's palette now lightened considerably; he had spent the summer of 1869 with Degas at Boulogne, and the beach scenes he painted there show a strong feeling for light and atmosphere. This new *peinture claire,* as it is called, also owed something to his friendship with Berthe Morisot, a talented member of the Impressionist group. His paintings of this period show none of the contrived quality of the previous studio works, and he largely abandoned the stark contrasts of light and dark and the perplexing compositions in favor of a more spontaneous approach — an attempt to catch the fleeting effects of light and water that so entranced Monet. Manet described his friend as the "very Raphael of water," adding that he had "an understanding of its mystery and of all its moods." Here he has attempted to catch something of the same effect, and he was to further his study of water on a brief trip to Venice in the following year, when he painted two highly Impressionist waterscapes.

Monet later recalled a summer afternoon in his garden, where Manet, "beguiled by the color and light, had begun a painting *en plein air* with the figures under the trees. During the session Renoir arrived. Captivated in his turn by the charm of the hour, he asked me for my palette, brushes, a canvas, and began to paint at Manet's side." The subject was Camille, now Monet's wife, and their son Jean. The couple in Manet's painting, standing on the river bank looking out at the moored boats, is probably one and the same. The subject matter is pure Impressionist. In Manet's work, figures usually form the main subject, but here the woman and child, seen from the back, are almost incidental, serving mainly to point up the real subject of the painting — the river. The broken brushwork, which conveys a sense of movement, is also in the Impressionist idiom, but the color, although light and bright, is not used in the Impressionist prismatic manner, nor does Manet seem concerned with a precise color notation. All the works painted by the three artists over this summer were executed rapidly, with a light, fluid application of paint, and this picture is no exception.

During the summer of 1874 Manet worked out of doors with Monet and Renoir, painting in Monet's garden and on the banks of the Seine. The influence of the Impressionists is evident in his treatment and choice of subject. The figures, usually of paramount importance in Manet's paintings, are here merely an incidental part of the landscape. But although he lightened and brightened his palette in response to his friends' theories, he did not restrict himself to primary colors, continuing to use black and some earth colors. Impressionism was largely concerned with rendering the fleeting effects of nature by means of touches of pure color that approximated to the way light broke up the shapes and planes. Manet found this approach interesting up to a point — and was to use Impressionist technique to spectacular effect in the *rue Mosnier* series (see page 45) — but light and atmosphere were not his main concern. Nor was the countryside his natural habitat. Unlike Monet, he was not a committed landscape painter, preferring to draw his inspiration from the drama of city life.

1

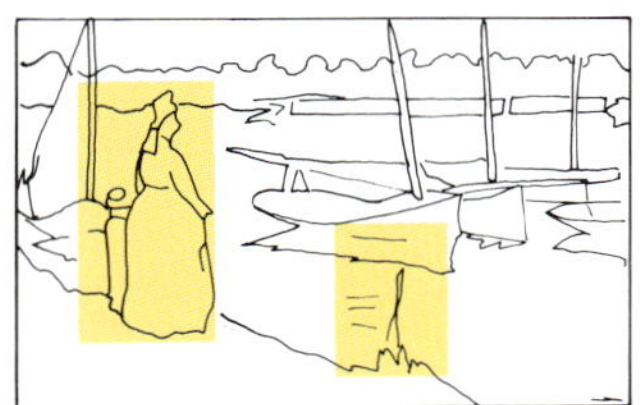

1 The models for the two figures were probably Camille and Jean, Monet's wife and child. Although painted largely in an Impressionistic style, the treatment of the hat is different, and stands in bold defiance of the Impressionist use of broken brushwork and prismatic color. Manet was master of the use of luminous black, and unlike the Impressionists, he never banished the color from his palette. Here he has used it to delineate the trim and ribbons of the woman's tilted hat. By contrast, the texture of her white dress is created by means of light touches of color laid on in vertical sweeps, suggesting both reflections of local color and the folds of the skirt's fabric.

2 *Actual size detail* Manet has used bold dashes of pure color to suggest the movement of water. Horizontal and diagonal strokes of unmixed cobalt and ultramarine create the overall local color, the glancing light is described by strokes of white, painted wet-in-wet, and yellow ocher, applied in diagonal brushstrokes, becomes the broken reflection of the boat's mast and rigging. The green clump of weed closest to the water shows the white canvas beneath and we can see both the fluid use of lighter color and a stiffer, drier use of darker pigment.

2 *Actual size detail*

Streetpavers in the Rue Mosnier

1878

25×31½in/63×79cm

Oil on canvas

Fitzwilliam Museum, Cambridge

From 1872-78 Manet occupied a studio on the first floor of 4 rue de St-Petersbourg (now rue de Leningrad) in Paris. It looked out onto the rue Mosnier, a newly constructed road in a residential quarter in the eighth *arrondissement.* Some months after this picture was painted, Zola, in his novel *Nana,* described the street as one of ill repute. "Mme Robert lived in the rue Mosnier, a new and silent street . . . without shop fronts, but with beautiful houses, with their narrow apartments, peopled by women. It was 5 o'clock. Along the deserted pavements, in the aristocratic peace of the tall white houses, the *coupés* [carriages] of the stockbrokers and merchants stood idly by, while men hurried past, raising their eyes towards the windows, where the women in dressing gowns seemed to wait."

Shortly before leaving the studio, Manet did a series of paintings of scenes observed from his window, all of which show a dazzling use of Impressionist technique. Although not a member of the Impressionist group, Manet admired their work and was influenced by many of their observations, one of which was that shadows were not simply dark patches to be depicted in dead grays or browns, but areas of pure color. Monet saw that shadows reflected their surroundings, and that the colors in them were the complementaries of those in the object which cast the shadow. In Manet's painting, the shadows cast by the afternoon sun are a pale violet-blue, complementary to the yellow of the street itself. This complementary color scheme is continued throughout the painting, with the pale, chalky yellow of the buildings shadowed by violet or broken up by shutters and balconies of the same color.

In 1867 Monet had painted a series of Parisian street scenes. These cityscapes are an urban version of his landscapes; figures are incidental, of equal importance to the clouds in the sky. Manet, by contrast, excludes the sky, concentrating on recording the "slice of life" glimpsed from his studio. For Monet, Paris was a pattern of changing light and atmosphere, but for Manet it was less a landscape than a place of social interest, endlessly opening new vistas for fascination and astonishment. Although using the Impressionist technique, he places the emphasis on the individuals and their activities, offering the possibility of interpreting the picture at least partially as social observation — never the case with Monet's works. The pavers are the ostensible subject of the scene, but the canvas also includes numerous visual references which enhance the impression of everyday life in the city. There is the hoarding on the left urging the purchase of fashionable children's clothing; the slumped figure on the pavement below; the cement mixer on the right, and a little scene of household removal down the road. If Zola is to be believed, the still, black carriages are the conveyances of the gentleman visitors to the ladies of the street.

The theme of Parisian life became one of increasing importance to Manet. The following year he approached the prefecture with the suggestion of decorating the new town hall with scenes of everyday life instead of the traditional allegories of the city. He wanted to show what he described as "the belly of Paris," the industry, commerce and public life of the day. "I would have Paris markets, Paris railways, Paris port, Paris underground, Paris racetracks and gardens." His proposal met with no response, but this painting gives an idea of what he might have done had his idea found favor with the authorities.

This work is a stunning example of Manet's ability to capture open-air light effects. It was painted on a canvas slightly smaller than the standard vertical landscape format of $32\times24\frac{1}{2}$in (81.25×62cm), but this is probably only because standard measurements varied marginally from one color merchant to another. The grain of the extra-fine canvas is visible through the paint in places, and the texture of the weave is exploited by dragged color in some areas of the painting. The ground is a pale gray tint, enhancing the overall effect of pale luminosity, and uniting the many creamy tints in the painting. There are none of the stark tonalities and harsh color juxtapositions of Manet's earlier work; all the colors are light and pastel-like, with lead white added to them to increase their light-reflectiveness.

1

2

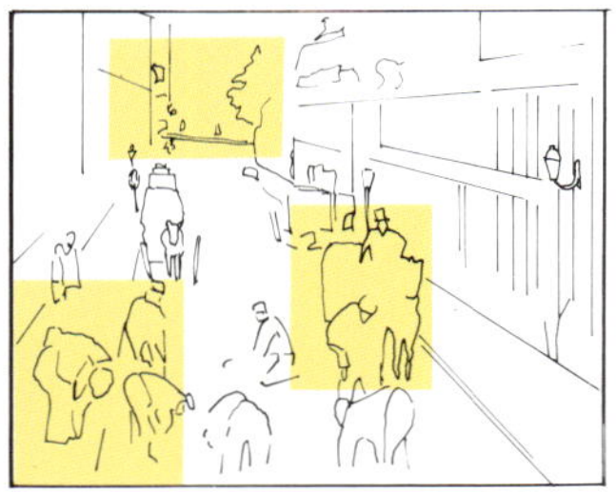

1 This detail shows the subtlety of the colors and tones very clearly: there are no dark shadows or dramatic contrasts of tone to break up the unity imposed by the sunlight. The effect of recession, with the colors becoming increasingly blue in the distance, is beautifully represented by the technique of rubbing a thin translucent veil of pale opaque blue over the stone colors. This has given a floating, insubstantial quality to the reflected light in the shadows.

2 Viewed from a distance, the figures of the streetpavers look solid and convincing, but this detail shows how freely the paint has been used, with no attempt at literal description. The paint has largely been applied wet-in-wet, so that colors and brushstrokes blend together. The loose handling and broad brushstrokes give a feeling of movement and immediacy to the scene. The blues and violets of the background appear again on the figures, with touches of a mixed orange providing a vivid contrast.

3 *Actual size detail* The stasis created by the enforced idleness of the driver waiting in the carriage contrasts with the activity of the workman immediately in front of him. Appropriately, the former is painted with a drier, less fluid application of pigment. The horse, carriage and driver are overlaid with short, thin brushstrokes of dark red, while the workman is more simply realized with a bolder, thicker application of paint applied wet-in-wet.

3 *Actual size detail*

Girl Serving Beer

1878-79

$30\frac{1}{2} \times 25\frac{5}{8}$in/77.5×65cm

Oil on canvas

Musée d'Orsay, Paris

The café lay at the heart of French social life, particularly towards the end of the last century, increasing in importance as a response to a rapidly growing urban population, often living in overcrowded, cramped conditions. The café provided more than simply relaxing and congenial surroundings in which to take a drink. It was the very center of metropolitan popular culture: a place where newspapers were read, letters written — and often received — old friendships kept up and new ones formed. Class differences were temporarily suspended, allowing the poorest laborer to rub shoulders with affluent men-about-town, and prostitutes to seek temporary refuge as well as clients. Most important for the artists and writers of the period was that cafés gave them somewhere to meet and discuss their work. Manet was closely associated with a number of Parisian cafés: in his twenties and early thirties he frequented the fashionable Café Tortoni and the literary Café de Bade; from 1866 he favored the Café Guerbois, where the proprietors reserved two tables every Thursday evening for "Manet's band"; and ten years later, the Café de la Nouvelle-Athènes became his preferred venue. The 1870s saw a new development, with the introduction of the café-concert, a light musical entertainment aimed at a working-class audience. Manet and Degas both based paintings on the theme of these popular concerts, and the café was also treated in literature, notably by Zola, whose *L'Assommoir* (1876-77) was widely circulated among Manet's circle.

This painting relates directly to the *Waitress Serving Beer* (opposite below), and the two are often confused. Both works show the same two principal figures, but in the London version they are placed inside a larger space, which includes a glimpse of the double-bass player, the dancer on stage, the marble counter cluttered with glasses, and a section of the clientele. The lower half of both figures is also visible. It is not known definitely which painting is the earlier, although it seems more likely that this is a later revision of the London work. X-ray photographs and traces of earlier painting *(pentimenti)* reveal that the London painting underwent many revisions in the course of its production. It is itself the right side of a larger picture which Manet cut in two (the left side is now in the Oscar Reinhart Collection, Winterthur, Switzerland.) A comparison between the two works suggests that Manet has, to use a photographic term, "zoomed in on the original shot," stripping extraneous detail for a more revealing close-up. The London version shows a busy barmaid deftly depositing glasses of beer with her right hand while looking across to her left, presumably toward the table where she is to take the remaining glasses. *Girl Serving Beer* focuses on the face of the woman herself, who engages us in the same way as did Victorine Meurent in *Déjeuner* (see page 25) and *Olympia* (see page 29), and prefigures the frontal gaze of the waitress in the *Bar at the Folies-Bergère* (see page 57).

The paint is handled with relish. Manet was a master of the seemingly effortless still life, giving flowers, fish and vegetables a freshness that makes them seem almost alive, and here the impression of two mugs of beer is created with consummate skill — no more than a few vivid strokes of freely handled paint. The waitress herself has a voluptuousness absent in the earlier work, a sensuality brought out by the delicious blue of her scarf and the charm of the flowered background which frames her. However many times Manet scraped down and repainted areas of a picture, he seldom failed to achieve the freshness and immediacy that was his ideal, and this painting, with its expressive brushstrokes and fluid lines, glows with life and animation.

Edouard Manet
Waitress Serving Beer
1878-79, National Gallery, London

Other related works show this establishment to be the Café Reichshoffen, and the model for the waitress, in both versions, was the actual serving girl at the café. The writer Théodore Duret recorded that "Manet had noticed the position of the waitress, who, while with one hand placing a beer on the table in front of a customer, knew how to hold several others in the other hand without spilling any . . . Manet approached the one at the café whom he believed the most skillful." The girl evidently agreed to go to Manet's studio in the rue d'Amsterdam on condition that her young man went with her, and it is he whom Manet has placed in the foreground, elbow on bar and smoking a pipe. It seems likely, although it is not known for certain, that the London version (left) was the earlier of the two.

1

2

1 The dramatic cropping of the stage performer was a device frequently used by Degas. Warm touches have been achieved by the use of a red halo effect which can be seen around the performer's left hand and on the left of the cool, bluish contour formed by the profile of the woman.

2 This detail shows the most freely worked area of the canvas. The overall blue effect of the man's smock has been created with bold sweeps of stiff Prussian blue overlaid with a lighter blue into which white and green have been worked more wetly. Long strokes of thickly applied white pigment have left a thin impasto line on either side of the brushstroke, suggesting the highlighted folds of the apron. The working-in of yellow ocher over the underpainting gives the impression of the semi-translucency of the glasses and of reflected local color.

3 *Actual size detail* The execution of the face is much tighter than that of other areas of the canvas. Like the waitress in *Bar at the Folies Bergere* (see page 57), the model here also has a high coloring. The deep pink tones of her mouth and the left side of her face are repeated in areas on either side of her. The tonal contrasts are relatively small, but white highlights have been used on the right side to indicate the source of light and also to give a luminosity to her complexion.

3 *Actual size detail*

NANA

1887
$59 \times 45\frac{3}{4}$in/150×116cm
Oil on canvas
Kunsthalle, Hamburg

Nearly fifteen years after the completion of *Olympia* (see page 29), Manet returned to the theme of the courtesan. Treated naturalistically, with no reference to the Old Masters, this painting takes as its subject a young actress-prostitute who was probably based on Zola's literary creation. Although the novel *Nana* was not published until the autumn of 1878, the character appears in the last part of Zola's *L'assomoir,* published in weekly instalments between 1876 and 1877. A contemporary critic, Félicien Champsaur, who knew both Manet and Zola, wrote of this, commenting on the way that Manet had painted Nana according to the impression given in the story, "aged eighteen, fully grown and already a prostitute. She is essentially a Parisienne, one of those women, plumply glowing with wellbeing, of delicate build, elegant or exciting."

The model was Henriette Hauser, mistress of the Prince of Orange, and like her sister Victorine, one of the well-known courtesans of the day. At that time such women were regarded more as princesses than as "ladies of easy virtue," and the figure of the crane on the Japanese screen may possibly be a reference to her status: *grue,* the french for crane, is also used as a designation for high-class prostitutes. It is tempting to read the male figure, cropped at the right side of the painting, as a representation of the ill-fated Baron Mouffard in *Nana,* who falls helplessly under the spell of the young actress. His tightly held cane suggests sexual tension, and possibly even sadistic practices. His erectly held head beneath the hat is balanced almost mockingly by the pot of flowers on the far left, while the rigidity of his pose is in sharp contrast to Nana's soft contours, which find their echo in the plump cushions and curves of the sofa.

At the same time, Degas was working on scenes of women in brothels, but his paintings have quite a different atmosphere. He chose lower-class women, showing them often in gross attitudes and treating them with the kind of impersonal scrutiny a biologist might show towards a new species of wild life. Manet was an admirer of women, and his appreciation of "La Citron" ("the Lemon"), as she was nicknamed, is shown in his naturalistic but delicate treatment. In contrast to the stark tonalities of his earlier work, this is painted with the light, bright palette beloved of the Impressionists, and the artist has clearly savored the quality of the paint itself, delighting in the recreation of the sumptuous fabrics and the glowing skin of the lovely young woman. But although certain parts of the canvas, notably the hem of the petticoat, the shoes and stockings and the slip on the chair, are entirely Impressionist in treatment, Manet has avoided their technique of broken brushwork in the areas of greater psychological importance, such as the two heads.

Submitted to the Salon of 1877, the painting was rejected as an affront to public morality. It was exhibited instead at Giroux, a curio shop, where crowds stood in line to catch a glimpse of it, and the outrage was so great that police intervention was nearly necessary. As in the case of *Olympia,* it was the subject rather than the way it was painted that caused offense. Nymphs or goddesses were acceptable and familiar, but here was a young *demi-mondaine* in the state of partial undress, and in the presence of a man of breeding. Worse still she seems to put the spectator in the position of interrupting the scene, turning her head as though to acknowledge our arrival. Manet can hardly have been surprised at the rejection, and the painting never found acceptance in his lifetime, remaining unsold until after his death. It then changed hands rapidly at an ever-increasing price until the director of the Kunsthalle, Hamburg, bought it in 1924 for 150,000 francs.

Centrally placed in the picture, the figure, modeled by a well-known model and actress of the day, dominates the canvas. The tilt of her head and the slant of her eyes direct us towards her companion, her expression hinting at a mocking disdain which is reinforced by the comic way he is portrayed.

The artist has delighted in displaying this *cocotte's* essential femininity, and has taken equal care with all the details of her dress and toilette, from the rouge and powder puff to the decorations on her shoes and stockings and the texture of the silk and lace of her underwear.

1 *Actual size detail*

1 *Actual size detail* This area at the upper left of the canvas provides an amusing visual counterpoint to the male head at the corresponding upper right side. The potted plant has been realized with a few freely painted blunt dabs of viridian overlaid with touches of bluish pink for the flower petals. A bright yellow has been used for the center of the flower, with the same color applied in thin strokes to highlight areas of leaf. The brass trim at the top of the green pot is created with a broad sweep of yellow ocher applied fairly stiffly over dry paint, with fine lines of yellow above and below.

2 Manet has used directional brushstrokes here to suggest falling shadow. The deep shade on the lower triangle of the cushion is achieved by a series of bold right-to-left diagonal sweeps of a densely applied darker green. The same technique has been used in modified form and with a light gray-blue to create the plump roundness of the buttocks.

3 The color of the stocking is echoed in Nana's underclothing, her discarded dress, and the painted wall decoration, the repetition of this clear, light blue pulling the canvas together. The detailing on the toe of the shoe is painted wet-in-wet, yellow over black.

2

3

Bar at the Folies Bergere

1881

$37^3/_4 \times 51^1/_4$in/96×130cm

Oil on canvas

Courtauld Institute Galleries, London

This was Manet's last great work, painted a year before his death. Seriously ill with locomotor ataxia, a degenerative disease of the nervous system which prevented him from moving with ease, his cast of mind was tending increasingly towards the melancholic. "Sorrow," he remarked, "is at the root of all humanity and all poetry." The painting is suffused with sadness as, isolated amid the splendor of the café, the young woman looks out with an unfocused and reflective gaze. The work draws together all the elements of Manet's work from the previous two decades: the contemporary subject matter, the single isolated figure, the idiosyncratic depiction of space, and the reference to a spectator beyond the picture plane. We are given, not only a demonstration of his virtuosity as a painter of still lifes, but also an invitation to probe beneath the surface at what remains always oblique and poetic.

Manet, who loved Parisian café life and the entertainments of the city, was drawn to fashionable haunts such as the now legendary Folies-Bergère, which opened in 1869. The novelist Huysmans described it as "stinking sweetly of corruption," seeing in such places a symbol of the times, and Guy de Maupassant was to describe the waitresses as heavily made-up women who "sold refreshments and love." But Manet's central figure has a freshness and innocence which recalls another literary source. She resembles Lisa, the *charcuterie* girl in Zola's novel *Le Ventre de Paris,* of which Manet owned an autographed copy. As Zola describes her standing behind her counter in the market of Les Halles, "she had a superb freshness, the white of her apron and sleeves continuing the white of the platters up to her rounded neck, to her rosy cheeks, where the tints of tender hams and pale translucent fats lived again . . . the mirrors . . . reflected her from the back, the front, the side . . . There a host of Lisas showed the breadth of shoulder, the full bosom, so still and soft that she aroused no carnal thought, and might almost have been a side of bacon." The high coloring and roundness of face certainly reflect Zola's description, and Manet's painting also emphasizes the same quality of being removed from her environment.

Isolated from the glitter of her surroundings, the expression of the waitress invites a multiplicity of interpretations, and is made still more ambiguous by the duality implied in the reflected image. Although the painting was received with acclaim at the 1882 Salon, its bizarre optical effects were commented on. The entire background presents a mirrored reflection of a gallery of seated figures, the counter of the bar at the front of the painting, and the waitress herself. Yet the reflection is deliberately inaccurate, not only in the positioning of the reflected figure but also in the pose, which shows her smaller and leaning slightly forward. Manet's denial of naturalism is provocative: he seems to have deliberately used the distorted reflection as a means of presenting another aspect of the subject.

Like *Olympia* (see page 29), this work involves the viewer directly. In the earlier painting, the hissing cat alluded to the arrival of an unseen visitor, and here the spectator is presented directly with himself in the form of the reflected male figure at the top right. In a contemporary caricature of the picture, the image was "corrected" by the inclusion of the back of this figure, deliberately excluded from the painting. The modernity of the setting and the simple grandeur and detachment of of the woman herself evokes one of Baudelaire's strictures on art. He held that the artist should interpret his own time while also recreating the magnificence of earlier art. "He must sift from fashion what is poetic in the historical, and extract the eternal from the transitory."

The Folies-Bergère was the embodiment of the type of establishment a contemporary Anglo-Saxon tourist guide warned against. "You cannot go into any public place in Paris without meeting one or more women that you will recognize at a glance as belonging to the class known in French society and fiction as the *Demi Monde.*" The model for the painting, whose freshness and innocence belies de Maupassant's description of the waitresses as heavily made-up women who sold "refreshments and love," was an actual barmaid at the establishment. Her name was Suzon, and she was doubtless picked for her prettiness. Manet posed her in his studio, where he had built a reconstruction of the marble bar, while the background, which includes a number of Manet's friends, was painted from studies made at the Folies-Bergère. The painter Gaston Latouche admitted to having posed for the gentleman on the right, while the woman in yellow gloves, recognizable from a pastel portrait, is the dazzling Méry Laurent, an intimate of the artist. Jeanne Demarsy, behind, in brown, has also appeared in portraits.

1

1 Manet has used painterly effects to create the texture of the model's hair, skin and clothing. The richness of the velvet costume has been achieved with a deep Prussian blue into which a lighter blue, or possibly white, has been worked in wetly to produce the effect of light on the folds of the fabric. For the lace trim of the dress, a transparent, thinned white has been laid lightly over the dark blue and then overlaid with denser swirls of pigment to suggest the patterns. The corsage of flowers picks up the girl's skin tones and echoes the still life motif in the foreground of the painting.

2 *Actual size detail* Manet painted a large number of fine still lifes, sometimes of nothing more than a loaf of bread, a few sticks of asparagus or a ham, and sometimes more elaborate flower pieces, which are among the loveliest of his paintings. This arrangement of two full blooms in a slender glass provides a delightful arrangement at the forefront of the picture as well as linking the immediate foreground to the figure of the girl in the center. The bottom of the glass above the stem is indicated by a bold sweep of stiff white pigment, while impasted white paint is used for the light-struck edges and top rim.

2 *Actual size detail*

3

4

3 Manet arranged the bottles and dish of oranges on the replica of the bar that he set up in his studio. Clearly identifiable are the bottles of champagne, crème de menthe and Bass Pale Ale, recognizable through its distinctive red triangle. The bottles are painted freely, wet-in-wet, while for the less reflective surface of the multi-faceted glass dish on the left, Manet has dragged white paint over a dry surface, highlighting the shiny skins of the mandarin oranges with small touches of thick white paint.

4 Clearly recognizable from other portraits is the celebrated beauty Méry Laurent, depicted here in yellow gloves. Kept by a series of wealthy men, she enjoyed the company of artists and musicians, and remained one of Manet's closest friends. Behind her, in beige, rapidly and sketchily painted, is Jeanne Demarsay, a young beauty whom Manet painted a number of times. The haze of smoke which de Maupassant described as hanging over the hall is suggested by the thin transparent overlay of blue paint. The fluid, free brushwork and lack of fine detailing of the seated figures, each realized with a few staccato strokes, evokes the bustle and animated chatter of the crowd in the gallery.

5

5 The smoke-dimmed mirrored reflection of the barmaid's back and the face of the man talking to her (who can only be seen in this reflection) have been laid in with thin paint and then overlaid with broad dashes of blue-gray paint, also thin. The barmaid is positioned immediately beneath a bright chandelier, and the sides of her head in the reflection are highlighted in pink, as are the cheekbones and nose of the man's face.

INDEX

Page numbers in *italic* refer to illustrations and captions

ACKNOWLEDGEMENTS

PHOTOGRAPHIC CREDITS

Bridgeman Art Library, London 11 bottom, 12; British Museum, London 25 bottom; Chicago Art Institute 6; Fitzwilliam Museum, Cambridge 45-47; Hubert Josse, Paris 7 bottom, 21-23, 25-27, 29-31, 33-35, 37-39, 49-51, 57-61; Kunsthalle, Hamburg 53-55; Kunsthalle, Mannheim 11 top; Musée de Dijon 7 top; National Gallery, London 17-19, 41-43, 49 bottom; National Gallery of Art, Washington 9 top and bottom; Prado, Madrid 8; Scala, Florence 29 bottom.